Leading
AND
Supervising
Instruction

To Bridget and Stephanie
And to the many great school leaders I have known

Leading
AND
Supervising
Instruction

JOHN C. DARESH

CORWIN PRESS
A SAGE Publications Company
Thousand Oaks, California

For information:

Corwin Press
A Sage Publications Company
2455 Teller Road
Thousand Oaks, California 91320
www.corwinpress.com

Sage Publications Ltd.
1 Oliver's Yard
55 City Road
London EC1Y 1SP
United Kingdom

Sage Publications India Pvt. Ltd.
B-42, Panchsheel Enclave
Post Box 4109
New Delhi 110 017 India

Printed in the United States of America

Library of Congress Cataloging-in-Publication Data

Daresh, John C.
Leading and supervising instruction/John C. Daresh.
     p. cm.
Includes bibliographical references and index.
ISBN 1–4129–0981–3 (cloth)—ISBN 1–4129–0982–1 (pbk.)
   1. Educational leadership-United States. 2. School supervision-United States.
3. School management and organization-United States. I. Title.
LB2805.D152 2006
371.2′03—dc22   2005037812

This book is printed on acid-free paper.

06   07   08   09   10   9   8   7   6   5   4   3   2   1

Acquisitions Editor:	Elizabeth Brenkus
Editorial Assistant:	Desirée Enayati
Copy Editor:	Jenny Withers
Typesetter:	C&M Digitals (P) Ltd.
Cover Designer:	Rose Storey

Contents

Preface

The past several years might be called "The Age of Accountability" in American public education. Beginning with individual state initiatives and reaching a crescendo with the adoption of No Child Left Behind legislation in the first George W. Bush administration, the emphasis in schools has clearly been directed toward finding ways to ensure taxpayers, parents, and political bodies that money spent in public education is money well invested. It has become the era of testing, testing, and even more testing.

Few would criticize the importance of schools demonstrating that they are doing what they can to ensure that all students are learning. And the efforts to ensure that, regardless of race, ethnicity, gender, or economic status, all children in all schools will achieve quality educational experiences is truly commendable. The problem is that, with such emphasis on demonstrable progress being so frequently shown through limited measures such as standardized achievement testing, other characteristics of effective schooling and learning might be placed in the "back seat." The net result for educational leadership is that many school administrators and supervisors now look at the goal of their work as directed almost exclusively at "getting the numbers up on tests each year."

The purpose of this book is to provide aspiring and practicing school leaders with a variety of other issues that may have an impact on the "numbers," but at the same time, serve as critical issues that will affect much more than the snapshots of schools provided by results of examinations each year. This is not to say that accountability issues must be ignored. But there is an even more critical element to effective leadership that each supervisor and administrator must address before starting special tutoring lessons, Saturday morning schools, "test camps," and other practices that have become increasingly popular in recent years as schools and school leaders have felt the pressure to perform.

The critical issue that we will examine through this book is the fact that all effective leaders begin with a common skill. That skill involves not managing testing, but rather managing personal values and beliefs.

Through the chapters of this book, you will be led to develop clear statements of your personal vision of how you look at teachers, motivation, and indeed, administration and leadership itself. The assumption made here is that, unless a leader comes to grips with these individualized perspectives, true learning directed by effective leadership will probably not occur in a school. Instead, the "leader" may run the risk of becoming little more than a manager of a school and testing activity.

Serving as an effective school leader today is a great challenge. Because of that fact, however, it makes opportunities for great satisfaction for achieving overall success an even greater source of pride and fulfillment than it may have ever been in the past. I hope that, as you develop your personal educational platform, your personal insights into what leadership really involves will grow along with your commitment to the most important contributions that effective schools can make to children, communities, and society in general.

ACKNOWLEDGMENTS

Over the years, I have been blessed with the opportunity to be able to learn from many great educators who know that the most important thing they do is to look at the needs of individual students and direct their energy toward addressing those needs. Nick Cobos, Armando Aguirre, Debbie Livingston, Jim Kelch, Carolyn Grantham, Ron Capasso, Sharon Camblin, and Mary Beth Cunat are among my personal "heroes" in the ways in which they have devoted their careers to providing effective leadership that is directed toward children, not personal survival. I thank them all for their advice, suggestions, examples, and above all, friendship and colleagueship.

Care and dedication to the real focus of effective schooling is not limited to my practitioner colleagues named above. At the university level, I have also been able to work with people like Rick Sorenson, Rodolfo Rincones, Kathy Whitaker, Nancy Evers, Bruce Barnett, Vern Cunningham, Gene Hall, Dick Andrews, Myrna Gantner, Karen Dunlap, Dick King, and dozens of other "higher ed types" who have never lost their dedication to the ideal of quality schooling being available to all children. My thanks to these and many others not named is a big part of my work.

Finally, I again note my appreciation for friends and colleagues at Corwin Press. Robb Clouse, Douglas Rife, and Lizzie Brenkus have all assisted me with their kindness, feedback, and patience over the years.

Corwin Press gratefully acknowledges the contributions of the following reviewers:

Dr. Bob Brower
Superintendent
North Montgomery Community School Corporation
Crawfordsville, TN

Jim Hoogheem
Retired Principal
Fernbrook Elementary School
Maple Grove, MN

Frank Kawtoski
Associate Faculty
Eastern University
St. David's, PA

Kermit Buckner, EdD
Professor
Department of Educational Leadership
East Carolina University
Greenville, NC

About the Author

 **John C. Daresh** is Professor of Educational Leadership at the University of Texas at El Paso. Over the years, he has held faculty or administrative positions at the University of Cincinnati, The Ohio State University, and the University of Northern Colorado. He has worked as a consultant for universities, state departments of education, professional associations, and individual schools and districts across the United States, and also in Canada, France, Holland, Israel, the United Kingdom, South Africa, and Taiwan. In addition to his university appointment, Daresh also serves the Chicago Public Education as the lead consultant on principal mentoring, a key component of the school district's commitment to the creation of more effective instructional leaders to serve the needs of the children of a great, world-class city.

1 Introduction

A New View of Supervision

Imagine two very different conceptualizations of what a school might look like. On the surface, these two perspectives might first appear to be quite similar. Both involve a pair of circles. Actually, each picture includes a small, inner circle surrounded by a larger one, almost as if there are two targets and two bull's-eyes. But, there are major differences between the two diagrams. In one, the large circle is entitled "The Needs of Students," while the smaller circle at the center carries the descriptor, "The Priorities of the School." In the second picture, the titles are reversed. The larger circle carries the description "The Priorities of the School" while the center circle says, "The Needs of the Students." The diagrams, at a distance, look the same. But as one approaches and examines the two diagrams, there is a world of difference.

In the real world of education, the same observations can be made about schools. They tend to all look pretty much alike. All have organizational structures, with classes, teachers, administrators, support personnel, classified staff, students, and parents. All schools exist and operate within certain communities and environments, complete with laws, governance patterns, financial parameters, and so forth. But, as most people—whether professional educators or members of the lay public—realize very quickly, there are significant differences between schools that often appear on the surface to be quite similar.

Like the "Tale of Two Circles" that opened this chapter, we often see situations that appear to be similar to others, but we quickly learn that distinctions often contribute to the quality of one setting over another. Two restaurants offer the same menu, but one restaurant is regarded as a place that serves great meals, while the other establishment has very little repeat business. Hotels seem to offer the same basic services, yet one place files for bankruptcy while its rival is classified as a "Five Star" hotel that draws continual rave reviews from guests.

Throughout this book, an assumption is made that, as a school leader, you are interested in ensuring that schools with which you are associated are perceived as "good schools" that deserve "Five Star" ratings and kudos from your clients. You want your school to be better than average, or a place that "makes a difference." Unlike the hotel operators or restaurateurs, you may not be concerned about making certain that you attract a lot of repeat customers or higher profits than your competitors. But, as an educational leader, you are vitally concerned about the importance that each and every one of your "customers" receives a positive experience. In your world, that is translated as learning, developing potential, and maintaining a positive self-image and quality of life.

This book is directed toward helping you achieve the goal of leading your school to become like the second circle described earlier. Instead of becoming the administrator or manager of a school where your role is simply one of requiring students to conform to the expectations and needs of the school, you will be provided with an alternative perspective that defines effective educational leadership as developing a school where the primary goal is always defined as putting the needs of learners at the center of all activity.

We will look at this approach to effective supervision through a number of different perspectives, both theoretical and practical. You will quickly appreciate an important assumption made here, and that is the fact that the kind of effort promoted here is not necessarily something that is easy to do immediately. The fact is, there are quite a large number of schools across the country that have operated for a long time using the model of the first circle, where learners must conform to the school. And this has been acceptable because there are many who view schools as nothing more than normative institutions that control student behavior. It may also be understandable because it is typically much easier to run an organization that always follows the same patterns for operating. On the one hand, if your goal is to run a school in a predictable, efficient, and uncomplicated way by doing little more than ensuring that all students comply with your rules, your regulations, and your needs for control, you find the whole premise of this book to be contrary to your own views and values.

On the other hand, if you believe that "schools are for kids" and "kids come first" are more than simplistic, overused slogans, you may find the following chapters to be very helpful to you in providing leadership in your school. In Chapter 2, for example, a number of different historical views of supervisory practice are offered. Each is likely to be a tempting definition for an important part of supervision in schools. Depending on which view you find most consistent with your personal assumptions, you may begin to recognize which of the "two circles" is what you wish to see in a school.

This book, in a sense, is all about the values of leaders. First, there is the overriding orientation described in this chapter. It says, quite simply, that the most critical issue for anyone in education—whether classroom teacher or school administrator—must involve directing all activities in any school toward the needs of students. That theme is introduced in every chapter of the book. In each case, after you read through material designed to assist you in developing a personal awareness of a specific issue faced by an educational supervisor, you will be asked to consider an important "So what?" question. Here, the question is always posed in reference to how the material introduced in a chapter can be consistent with the overarching theme of "children at the center of the circle." If you are not convinced that the driving force of a good school must be the needs of students, reading this book may be quite an uncomfortable experience for you.

Second, regardless of the type of organization, the most critical thing to be understood by an effective leader will always be his or her value orientation in the first place. Simply directing a school toward achieving high test scores each year will eventually become a meaningless, mechanical activity if the principal is not fundamentally convinced that student learning must be ensured, and that testing is a way to see if that goal is still in front of the school. In other words, if the leader does not truly value something, those expected to follow will be unlikely be swayed to perform stated goals and objectives.

Noting the importance of understanding personal leadership values has led many to suggest that a critical duty of anyone seeking success as a leader must be the periodic reflection on personal perspectives and orientation to issues that one will face as a leader. Argyris (1982) and later Sergiovanni and Starratt (1993) have noted that a leader's actions are guided when they are imbedded as part of a personal philosophy of action. In each chapter of this book, you will be asked to pause and reflect on the content that is presented, and measure that in terms of its effect on your personal values. By the conclusion of this book, it is expected that you will have considered many "planks" that traditionally constitute a platform statement.

The book is divided into three sections that are related to broad themes that need to be addressed by a leader developing a personal educational platform. The first section ("Views About the Job") contains individual chapters that address your perceptions of various characteristics of administration and supervision in general. Chapters will ask you to reflect on issues that are related to certain realities that provide a fundamental definition of effective leadership. Chapter 2 challenges you to reflect on several possible traditional perspectives and alternative models as you develop a personal response to the question "What is supervision?" Chapter 3 then asks you to define "leadership" in terms that are consistent with your platform. In subsequent chapters, you will be invited to focus on many specific aspects of leading a school. You will reflect on what the concepts of power and authority mean to you as a fundamental reality of serving as a leader (Chapter 4) and how to deal with conflict (Chapter 5).

The second section of the book ("Views About the People Who Make Up a School") asks you to consider your stance concerning the "people side" of your world as a leader. For example, Chapter 6 presents information about the realities of the lives of teachers and asks you to assess your real views of who teachers are and how you value their work. Evaluation is a term often associated with supervisory practice, and so we look at it with a recognition that supervisors must come to some personal judgment of what their role is to be. That will be the central theme considered in Chapter 7. The last two chapters ask you to consider your personal stance regarding such matters as how to define effectiveness (Chapter 8) and the purpose of schooling (Chapter 9).

Each chapter follows the same basic pattern as it addresses its content. In every case, a brief case study will introduce the major issue of the chapter. Next, information concerning the main topic is provided to you in a way that asks you to participate in reviewing certain key concepts. In a section on building your platform, you will be invited to think about your personal responses to each of the points raised throughout the chapter. Every chapter includes a section in which you are provided with some ideas of how you might be able to apply what you have read to your work as an effective school leader.

This book supports the notion that educational leaders who are most successful have a clear sense of the purposes of schooling in general. They also have developed clear personal philosophies concerning the nature of the people with whom they work each day. And they have constructed a sense of purpose and reality in terms of the nature of the job of being a school leader in the first place. Effectiveness is based on the ability to do tasks and carry out responsibilities correctly. But it is also important that leaders construct a personal sense of why they do what they do in the first place.

School leaders are important people because they can create the conditions that are necessary to make schools into learning places, not simply buildings where students are "warehoused" each day. You can appreciate that a number of key concepts will assist you not only in carrying out your assigned responsibilities in an orderly and effective fashion but, more important, acquiring insights into ways in which your work will have as great an impact as possible on learners.

IN REVIEW

Effective supervision and administration in education is to be directed toward the creation and maintenance of good schools. In turn, good schools are defined as those in which all efforts are made to support the needs of students. Too often, schools are operated as if the most important objective is to coerce students into complying with the expectations of the schools.

REFERENCES

Argyris, C. (1982). *Reasoning, learning, and action: Individual and organization*. San Francisco: Jossey-Bass.
Sergiovanni, T. J., & Starratt, R. J. (1993). *Supervision* (5th ed.) New York: McGraw-Hill.

PART I

Views About the Job

2 Understanding Approaches to Supervision

B ob Clarke and Bridget Carson had known each other for several years. They attended State University together, they student taught together, and they both had their first teaching jobs in the same school district. In fact, they even worked in the same school, Elm Street Elementary, for two years. They both finished graduate studies at State at the same time and received their credentials as school administrators in the same year. Bridget found an administrative job—assistant principal at a middle school—a year before Bob did, but both were assistants in the district for five years. Coincidentally, Bridget and Bob applied for and were appointed for principalships in the district at two different schools at the same during the summer. They now found themselves in the same small group at the County Administrators "New School Year" meeting. The subject was "How can we be the kind of principals who promote success for our students?" and they were each asked to describe the ways in which they planned to provide effective leadership and direction in their schools the next year.

Not surprisingly, the veteran principals in the group made a few jokes about the assignment and some clearly "tuned out" for the remainder of the small group sharing session. But Bob and Bridget were both eager to get started in their new professional roles. They were very interested in the discussion that had been initiated to ask each small group to consider the "best ways" for principals to address the newest state mandates for increased attention by building principals to monitoring student achievement. The directions for each group required each participant to describe the strategies that they intended to follow in preparing teachers in their schools to address the new state vision. Bob and Bridget had initially been assigned to different small groups, but they decided to break the rules of the facilitator in order to stay together. As rookies, they decided that it would be interesting to hear each other's ideas on the subject.

The other two principals in the small group simply indicated that the approach they would likely take would be just to sit back and allow the state's department to clarify what they actually meant by the new standards that were to be addressed in local schools. As Adrian Sanchez noted, "I never get too excited about trying to explain bureaucratic proclamations to my staff. Who knows how long this stuff is going to last anyway."

The two newcomers decided that, despite the insights shared by their senior colleagues, the discussion question would be worth considering by rookies who had yet to direct teachers at this point. Bridget started the conversation.

"The first thing I plan to do as principal, regardless of any state mandate about testing or anything else, is to make sure that my teachers know what I expect. I know that there's a lot of talk about how critical it is for principals to work with teachers as colleagues and seek consensus about what's going on in a school. But let's be honest. My neck is on the block as the new principal, and the knife that will be used on all of us will be sharpened by the requirements of the state accountability system. We can't afford to sit around and discuss the inevitable. My teachers are going to do what they do best, namely teach, and my job is going to be to clearly indicate how they are to teach, and to what end."

"Wow!" said Bob. "You certainly have a very clear sense of what you want to do, and how you want to do it. It's not a path that I want to follow. The way I plan to approach this issue is quite a bit different. What I plan to do is get to know my teachers first, then after we all get on the same page, I don't think it will be quite as difficult to get people involved in the new expectations of the state. I fully believe in the notion that 'happy teachers make a happy school, and a happy school is a good school.'"

The two beginning principals kept up their conversation for the remainder of the small group session. Meanwhile, the experienced principals in the group sat back and smiled.

People who are leaders come from many different backgrounds. There are women who grew up in small towns with very conservative political views. And there are African American men who come from middle-sized communities where the traditional political talk took on a more liberal tone. People from both groups become school principals. Above these rather obvious distinctions, there are other factors that contribute to the diversity of leadership practices seen in schools across the nation each day.

The greatest differences that one may likely see are not derived from gender, ethnicity, childhood experiences, nationality, economic level, or race. Rather, school leaders all have very different points of view concerning what the most important parts of their jobs ought to be.

✦✦✦

In this chapter, different perspectives that have been followed in the administration and leadership of schools are considered. While some of these perspectives may appeal to you because they resonate with some of your personal values and beliefs, other perspectives may seem almost improper or distasteful. The point of what is described here is not to preach that one set of beliefs and assumptions is necessary better than others. However, while you may review these different management philosophies and select one or another view as more appealing, recall that the real focus is constant. This book is all about upholding the clarity of one central belief, which is that overriding perspective of any educational leader must always be that the needs of learners should drive your actions. Kids do come first.

Before going any further with a discussion regarding the foundations of educational leadership and supervision, it may be important to consider an important issue facing you, and that is your personal response to the question "What is supervision?"

This book takes the view that supervision is much more than identifying the best ways to go about observing and analyzing what takes place in a teacher's classroom for the purpose of evaluating performance. Supervision is much more than learning how to maintain control over teachers as employees. In these days, when serving as an effective educational leader has come to include a multitude of complex and often competing demands and tasks, it is extremely hard to pigeonhole effective supervision as a crisp and distinct activity that is defined clearly as work directed at only a few activities in schools. It is important to stop and think about some of the personal assumptions that may already be shaping your view of what supervision is or "ought" to be.

In the following space, write your personal definition of "educational supervision." In your definition, you may wish to include some of the most critical things that an educational supervisor is expected to do on a regular basis.

_____

_____

_____

_____

_____

_____

_____

Your personal definition may include some issues common to supervision in education and supervision in the corporate and industrial world. No doubt, in many cases, teacher evaluation has been noted as central to a definition of "supervision." In some other places, you might have noted that supervisory personnel are involved in the process of checking staff and teacher time cards, lesson plans, or attendance records. In this way, you may have touched on an area of supervision that has been consistent with some historical perspectives that have been identified through the literature on the topic of supervision in school for many years (Daresh, 2002). Four of these perspectives are considered here.

1. *Supervision as inspection.* In this view, supervisors are meant to devote most of their time and attention to finding out what is wrong with what teachers are doing in their classrooms (assuming that what teachers are doing is mostly wrong!). The second feature of this perspective is that the supervisor has the responsibility of intervening directly in the work of teachers to correct faulty performance.

At first glance, it would appear that following the model of inspection represents a complete lack of trust in teachers as professionals. In terms of current criticisms of management practice, this view of supervision might be compared with micromanagement, where the administrator demonstrates a view suggesting that subordinates are so incapable of effective performance that the manager must intervene and control employees very directly. It is as if the motto of the leader could be, "Since the people hired are so incompetent, you have to do it yourself." It may be of interest to note that the image of the educational supervisor as an inspector was very popular during the earliest period of formal schooling in the United States. As schools became established across the nation in the 17th, 18th, and 19th centuries, teachers often had little formal training to prepare them to work with pupils. The curriculum of most schools was quite limited and typically focused on little more than basic skill development in reading, writing, and arithmetic—the "Three R's." Even with such a narrow perspective, however, it was often doubtful if those who were employed as teachers knew much more than the students with whom they worked. As a result, more experienced teachers often took on the duty of providing basic oversight to ensure that what was going on in classrooms represented some quality of instruction. Teachers were often presumed to be limited in their knowledge, and that presumption was often warranted. Those who engaged in oversight, or supervision, of instructional practice were understandably subject to inspection and micromanagement of their work.

In schools today, an administrator or supervisor who believes in the value of using inspection as an approach to leadership would probably spend a great deal of time engaged in direct observation of teachers for the purpose of making certain that what teachers were doing in their classrooms conformed to district or state guidelines and expectations. While there is nothing inherently sinister about principals doing many "walkthrough" observations of teachers, a person who would define her or his role as an inspector would be in classrooms largely because of a concern that what teachers were doing was generally inappropriate and needing some oversight by a person of authority.

Other actions guided by an administrator or supervisor who believes in the need for inspection might be spending a good deal of time in the front office of the school each day to ensure that teachers were showing up for work at the assigned time, checking classrooms after the school day ends each day to see if teachers were leaving the school earlier than permitted, and so forth. In some schools, principals have installed time clocks in the main office and have required teachers to "punch in" and "punch out" each day. Careful accounting of time spent at work would be a sign that teacher behavior was being inspected, as would the expectation that teachers would turn in detailed lesson plans each week for administrative review and approval.

The decision by an individual to inspect the work of teachers is not completely one based on personal philosophy or preference. To a large extent, the actions of educational administrators are defined by state, district, or even national policies and laws. School administrators are held accountable for the actions of teachers who are under contract to begin their work day at a certain time each day. Local school systems may have policies requiring teachers to furnish proof of their dedication to quality education by providing lesson plans on a regular basis. And states and the federal government are increasingly asking school leaders to engage in careful monitoring of teacher activity as it relates to student achievement. Whether or not an individual principal wants to supervise as an inspector, this responsibility will likely continue be an integral part of the job of leading a school.

On the other hand, "supervision as inspection" also implies a personal choice of how to serve as a principal or assistant principal in a school, apart from the expectations of "No Child Left Behind" or state legislation calling for tight accountability. The inspection perspective suggests that a supervisor may likely have some fundamental assumptions regarding the trustworthiness of teachers in the school. These assumptions are likely to guide much of what the supervisor does and how he or she does it.

Describe how a school leader who subscribed to the beliefs of the inspection model of supervision might carry out some traditional duties. For example, how might an "inspector" go about evaluating staff?

_____

_____

_____

_____

_____

_____

_____

2. *Supervision as a "scientific" activity.* Here, the supervisor is defined largely as an "efficiency expert" or manager endowed with the special expertise that would enable him or her to provide the "research-based" and "correct" answers to every possible problem encountered by employees. And it was because of this special expertise and knowledge that the scientific manager's role was set aside from the work of everyday, common employees.

Toward the end of the 19th century, America moved quickly from the traditions of an agrarian society to an industrial world. Cities increased in size, and social institutions such as schools raced to keep up with that growth. At the same time, the economies of western nations moved toward reliance on industry and manufacturing of durable goods. It was a time when there was a discovery of the power of mass production through mechanization. This focus on efficiency in industry influenced many other aspects of the lifestyles of the time, including social institutions such as schools. It was much more efficient (and therefore, "sensible") to create larger schools where many students could be taught standardized subjects by specially trained educational professionals.

Teachers were suddenly viewed as workers needing training to prepare them for the new vision of education that was emerging across the nation. Training focused on helping individuals learn the "proper" methods of instruction and ways of working with young people. While teachers were acquiring specialized skills in the craft associated with their work in classrooms, the increasing complexity and size of schools called for the creation of a new class of professional managers to ensure the coordination of activity within bigger schools. The era of trained school managers and administrators emerged.

These approaches to educational practice were influenced strongly by practices and beliefs that were being honed in the larger society of the late 19th and early 20th centuries. "More is better" and "more produced faster is cheaper" were beliefs expressed by leaders in the industrial world. The assembly line became the way in which goods were being produced all over the western world. And a new management philosophy was born to assist in the development of more efficiency and greater productivity.

When you stop and think about several issues, it is easy to understand the reasons why practices used in producing low cost products for the masses might well be adopted by those responsible for managing schools. This was particularly true in the late 19th and early 20th centuries, when so many moved from rural communities to larger cities. Small schoolhouses disappeared and much larger school buildings became the norm. Where hundreds of students were now being housed under one roof, it became necessary to find ways to manage this greater complexity. Techniques used to administer large factories became useful in educational administration.

Those seeking ways to manage education found theories in the corporate world quite appealing. Among the writers of the time who were able to offer reasonable hope for managers was Frederick Winslow Taylor, an industrialist now frequently referred to as the "Father of Scientific Management." He identified several practices that would enable organizations to be managed much more effectively and efficiently (1916):

- *Time study principle.* (All productive effort should be measured by accurate time study and a standard time established for all work done)
- *Piece rate principle.* (Wages should be proportional to output and their rates based on the standards determined by the time study. As a corollary, a worker should be given the highest possible grade of work)

- *Separation of planning from performance principle.* (Management should take over from workers the responsibility for planning the work and making the performance possible. Planning should be based on time studies and other data related to production, which are scientifically determined and systematically classified; it should be facilitated by standardization of tools, implements, and methods)
- *Scientific methods of work principle.* (Management should take over from workers the responsibility of their methods of work, determine scientifically the best methods, and train the workers accordingly)
- *Management control principle.* (Management should be trained in and taught to apply scientific principles of management and control)
- *Functional principle.* (The strict application of military principles should be reconsidered, and their industrial organization should be so designed that is serves the purpose of improving the coordination of activities among the specialists)

What are some examples of how "scientific management" practices are still followed extensively in schools today?

_____

_____

_____

_____

_____

_____

_____

Your list of current school-based applications of scientific management might include obvious examples such as the fact that there is a clear separation of "administrative duties" from "teaching responsibilities" in most schools. Teachers teach, but administrators manage. This is reinforced by the specialized preparation of school administrators by pursuing academic degrees and licensure that emphasizes management skill development rather than teaching practice. These are neither "good" nor "bad" features of the "scientific" approach we have taken in the design of modern schools. But they are clear indicators of how one perspective of supervisory practice (i.e., scientific management) has had a major impact on the ways in which we operate education in the United States today.

3. *Supervision as a human relations activity.* From this perspective, supervisors are primarily responsible for engaging in behavior that would contribute to feelings of satisfaction, well-being, and personal happiness among employees. This is a view that strongly suggests that the most productive employees are those who are happy, and the job of a supervisor is to make people happy.

It is not surprising to discover that, after years of "supervision" being defined as a form of inspection or in quasi-scientific terms, an alternative view of how to lead in organizations would emerge. Human relations management should not be confused with a basic principle of organizational behavior that holds that, regardless of overall practice and perspective, managers must somehow acknowledge the needs of individuals who work in their organizations. In other words, it is important always to show an appreciation of basic human needs. Even in the case of supervision as a form of inspection, those who act as administrators must demonstrate attitudes indicative of caring and respect for others. Often, it is assumed that supervision as "inspection" or "scientific management" is typified by the behavior and attitudes of Ebenezer Scrooge in *A Christmas Carol*. The key issue with the perspectives described earlier is that the primary goal for supervisors was to focus almost exclusively on organizational priorities and needs rather than employee issues. But that does not necessarily result in inhumane treatment by managers.

The perspective of supervision as a human relations activity states in large measure that a critical concern of anyone in an administrative position is the ability to ensure that workers are happy with their efforts. The reason for this is not entirely based on a concern for personal needs. Rather, it is based on the belief that, when employees are happy and satisfied, they will become more effective in their work habits. As a consequence, the productivity of organizations will increase. Oddly enough, this "human relations perspective" does not necessarily depend on managers possessing fundamentally good human relations skills.

In a school where human relations supervision is practiced, there are likely to be many signs that the intent of ensuring a sense of personal comfort and satisfaction is present among the staff. It would be likely that the principal might engage in a great deal of personal contact with teachers. Numerous complements regarding teacher performance would be heard. "Teacher of the Week" (or "Month" or even "Day") designations might be common, and in many cases, notes of congratulations might be found frequently in teachers' mailboxes.

The kind of school described here might be attractive to many educators. A great deal of energy is directed toward the "people side" of the organization. Most observers might suggest that there is very little not to appreciate in a "human relations" type of work environment. But there are certain shortcomings. For example, in a school with anywhere from 30 to more than 200 teachers, it is unlikely that the same techniques of "making people feel good about their work" will be viewed with equal favor by everyone on the staff. A note of congratulations for one teacher might be viewed very positively, but the same note for another staff member can be interpreted as a disingenuous action. Another criticism of management directed primarily at satisfying the emotional needs of employees has been that this perspective is often dishonest or even manipulative. Some would claim that trying to make everyone happy all the time is not only futile, it is dishonest. For each person who is honored, another can feel slighted.

Regardless of the positive or negative perceptions of relying on human relations skills as a way to lead, many school administrators rely heavily on this approach. In the space below, describe how you have observed one or more school leaders making use of a fundamental belief in the value of human relations management as the preferred method of leading a school.

_____

_____

_____

_____

_____

_____

4. *Supervision as human resource development.* This view is not wholly disconnected from the human relations view in that both perspectives suggest that an important role of any supervisor is to ensure that employees are satisfied and content. The major difference, however, is that human relations advocates look at making people happy as a prime goal so that, as an effect, organizations will become more productive. By contrast, the human resource manager strives to make the organization as successful and effective as possible, with the assumption being that productivity will result in greater employee satisfaction.

Human relations and human resource supervision have dual goals of ensuring that employees are satisfied and that the goals of the organized are achieved. The primary difference between them is found in the emphasis: a focus on employee needs as the primary outcome, or organizational productivity as the most important goal.

Human resource management makes several assumptions about the ways in which things ought to work. First, according to this view, if people are productive, they will be happy. If workers can achieve the goals that have been set out for their organizations, they will be satisfied because the principal reason people work is to accomplish something that they value personally. As a result, the supervisor becomes very interested in bringing about greater organizational effectiveness, thereby creating a setting where employees can feel satisfied through their association with productivity. In a school setting, this might mean that the leader focuses most of her or his energy on making certain that, for example, student performance in standardized achievement tests is very high, because this will make the teaching staff, as professional educators, feel as if professional and personal goals are being achieved.

Second, human resource development suggests that workers can be trusted to act professionally. Human resource management makes an important fundamental assumption that workers will be satisfied if they are productive, because people want to accomplish certain professional goals. People go into teaching largely because they want to see children grow, learn, and acquire skills. As a result, the most central motivating factor in the lives of those who work in schools will likely be the extent to which school goals are achieved. While teachers want to be treated with dignity and respect, the supervisor achieves that goal by treating them as if they are vital contributors to the effective school and not simply by providing short-term compliments and "strokes" in the same ways as one might witness in a human relations oriented school. Of course, there are other educators who do not necessarily view their work in the same light as professionals who are driven by such goals as the attainment of student achievement as a focus of their satisfaction. Some teachers look at their service as educators as simply a "job." As a result, these individuals might need a very different type of supervision to ensure that they are at least doing their job competently. In such cases, it may be naïve to assume that promoting productivity will automatically have the effect of satisfying most employees.

Describe some of the ways in which an educational leader who follows the human resource development perspective would go about working with the staff of a school.

What are some specific behaviors that you are likely to notice?

_____

_____

_____

_____

_____

_____

_____

WHICH PERSPECTIVES KEEP STUDENTS "AT THE CENTER"?

The primary purpose of this book is to provide a view of leadership in education where the supervisor's focus is truly directed at the needs of students. This chapter has considered the question of what supervision as a field of practice is all about. Four alternative perspectives of supervision were presented: Supervision as inspection, supervision as a scientific activity, human relations supervision, and human resource development. Each of these approaches is built on certain beliefs regarding the nature of students, teachers, and education in general. All four perspectives also have inherent assumptions regarding the purpose of management and desired outcomes of organizations. In other words, the approach that is often taken by any supervisor or leader is a part of the individual's personal philosophy. That issue will be considered in greater detail in the next chapter. But here, the focus is directed toward looking at whether or not the basic philosophy of an educational supervisor may be consistent with the overarching notion that the duty of a supervisor in schools must be to ensure that what goes on in schools is likely to benefit students.

Inspection

The first reaction that many educators have when they consider the notion that some educational leaders spend most of their time "inspecting" the work of teachers is understandably negative. After all, teachers justifiably view themselves as well-trained, competent, and professional. They assume that they will be treated with dignity and respect. But the idea that they are to be "inspected" as if they might be deficient, incompetent, and untrustworthy is very difficult to understand.

The fact is, most teachers deserve the kind of respect sought by many who work in schools. However, another fact is that there are, indeed, some teachers who need considerable oversight. Carl Glickman (2003) refers to these individuals as "teacher dropouts" or "unfocused workers" because they simply do not demonstrate the fundamental abilities associated with serving as effective teachers. They need a very directive approach by a supervisor or administrator. In Glickman's work, he identifies the following activities as appropriate for teachers who do not necessarily deserve the trust that might be shown to more accomplished teachers:

- *Directing*. The supervisor details simply and exactly what the teacher must do in order to address a problem and improve performance.
- *Standardizing*. The supervisor explains to the teacher what must be done in order to comply with the behaviors of all others in the school.
- *Reinforcing*. The supervisor specifically delineates the conditions and consequences for the teacher's improvement.

While the use of inspection, or the use of directive supervisory practice, may not be viewed in a positive light by many teachers, it may be a necessary strategy to use in some cases where the focus on student learning ("putting students at the center of the circle") is forgotten by some teachers. An educational supervisor may not make extensive or regular use of inspection, and it may be contrary to general views of teacher competence to choose a supervisory approach that suggests that a teacher is not to be trusted. But there may be some occasions when a teacher (or some teachers) are not truly indicating behavior that is in the best interest of students. Or there may be situations where some teachers are simply not competent to carry out their assigned responsibilities. In such cases, focus on the central vision of focusing on student needs may call for behavior that is apart from the normal approach to supervision that a leader might select.

In your experiences in schools, have you identified situations where the use of supervisory inspection might be the most appropriate strategy to be used to promote consistent attention to the needs of students in a school?

Provide examples.

_____

_____

_____

_____

_____

_____

_____

Scientific Supervision

The assumptions of scientific supervision state that, for organizations to work effectively, it is critical that those who are managers make most decisions and then communicate those decisions to employees. In this way, organizations will operate more efficiently and effectively. In schools, this would suggest that the principal or other administrators would function best by not involving teachers in making needed decisions. Like the use of inspection as a way to lead schools, reliance on the scientific approach to leadership might seem quite contrary to desired practice in education. Indeed, a fundamental view of the Educational Leadership Constituent Council (ELCC) Standards recently adopted by many professional associations representing the development of educational leaders has adopted participative management as a central guiding concept to be promoted among educational leaders:

> STANDARD 1: A school administrator is an educational leader who promotes the success of all students by facilitating the development, articulation, implementation, and stewardship of a school or district vision of learning that is shared and supported by the school community. (Wilmore, 2002, p. 19)

This Standard suggests that a primary responsibility of any school leader is to ensure the success of all students (by placing students at the center), and that a way to make this happen is to make certain that the leader engages in behavior that solicits input from all in a school. As a result, it would at first appear that a management philosophy that espoused the view that administrators should make all important decisions would be wholly inconsistent with the pursuit of effective leadership in schools.

The question must still be considered whether it is conceivable that, at times, the most effective strategy of a leader who wishes to ensure attention to student needs may require unilateral administrative decision making. The efficiency of scientific management may be the best way to make certain that needs of students are effectively addressed. As an example, consider the times when opportunities for grants and financial support may exist to enable schools to create new learner-centered programs. It may not be possible to engage in the type of consensus-building exercise that a leader may wish to follow in principle.

It is critical to note that scientific management is simply an alternative management strategy that does not necessarily reflect a leader's trust of employees, or a desire to work effectively with staff. The key, as we have noted throughout this description, is that the overriding value of anything must still be the needs of students if effective supervision is to take place.

In what situations might it be appropriate for a student-centered leader to make use of scientific management as a way to ensure that student needs are met?

_____

_____

_____

_____

_____

_____

_____

Finally, scientific approaches to supervision imply that there are "correct" answers to very important and complex questions that face educators. Why are some schools better than others? Do additional financial resources lead to greater student learning? Are teachers working as hard as they should to ensure student learning? These are but a few of the questions posed by professional educators as well as the lay public in general. And they are the foundation of the accountability movement of recent years that have led to the passage of No Child Left Behind legislation and policy at the national level, and high stakes achievement testing, standards-based curriculum development, and competency testing of teachers and administrators at the state level across the country. All of these measures have their roots in the assumptions and beliefs of an industrial society that was defined in large measure by adherence to the beliefs of scientific management. There is little doubt that educational leaders will be increasingly called upon to understand the assumptions of scientific supervision and its promise to provide "absolute" answers. The challenge of making certain that true focus on the needs of individual students will not be compromised will be a great one in years to come.

Human Relations

Scientific and inspection approaches to supervision call occasionally for an alternative perspective on the nature of educator responsibilities. If the prevailing philosophy of administration of a school has been founded on the principles of inspection and science for many years, it is understandable that the staff of that school may need to perceive a change of attitude. Consider a recently described case where the teachers in a middle school had consistently heard the message from two principals in a row who took an approach that suggested that teachers were not to be trusted, and that "anyone who does not get on board" with the principal "had better start to seek a transfer to another school." After eight years of such treatment, it was clear that the low morale of teachers needed to change. That change came along with the appointment of a new principal who spent most of his time assuring teachers that they were valued and respected.

The ideal approach to supervision taken in this book is that good practice is defined largely by the extent to which all energy in a school is directed primarily at the needs of students. Since the human relations perspective places great emphasis on the importance of leaders serving the needs of the people in an organization, some may assume that the ideal approach to learner-centered practice would be through the application of a human relations model. Such is not necessarily the case, however. There are, to be sure, many good reasons for a leader trying to satisfy the needs of workers and others. For example, in a case such as the one noted earlier where the previous school principals had made use of management practices that tended to ignore the interests of teachers, the person who followed the earlier administrators probably would have been well advised to spend a great deal of time learning about the wishes and interests of teachers as a way to change former operating procedures. Often, organizations need a clear reversal of past practice to enable a change of attitude and direction.

On the other hand, human relations management and supervision may not be needed in many schools. There may be many different ways for the leader to move the school toward greater sensitivity toward student needs.

List some of the ways in which an emphasis on human relations may be an effective way for the supervisor to move a school toward satisfying student learning needs more effective.

_____

_____

_____

_____

_____

_____

Human Resource Development

The final framework that we considered in our effort to define "supervision" was human resource development, where the fundamental assumption has been that the best way to ensure that teachers and other workers will be satisfied with their work is to enable them to achieve important personal and professional goals. Some might prefer this perspective to the others because it appears to enable leaders to focus equally on the needs of the organization and also the needs of workers. However, the best supervisory practice does not make use of only one approach under all circumstances. Human resource development makes an assumption that employees will be satisfied if they are able to achieve important professional goals. Unfortunately, not all teachers are driven by well-defined professional goals. In some cases, assuming that all teachers will be happy if their students succeed may be an incorrect belief. In some cases, teachers may need the oversight afforded by inspection. Taxpayers may need the "data-based" assurances provided through the application of scientific management. And there are schools, teachers, and whole communities that are "shell shocked" by administrators who ignored the "human side" of schooling, and so they now need an emphasis on strong human relations.

Under what circumstances would the application of human resource development be the most appropriate way to encourage a student-centered focus in schools?

_____

_____

_____

_____

_____

_____

BUILDING YOUR PROFESSIONAL PLATFORM

After reviewing the contents of this chapter, describe your basic views of an acceptable perspective of educational leadership. You may select one of the models described here, or you may combine elements from different models, including ones that you may know from your reading and study beyond this book.

_____

_____

_____

_____

_____

_____

IN REVIEW

This chapter reviewed four alternative perspectives of management as a way to try to develop different ways of understanding what supervision involves in the field of education. The perspectives included "inspection," where supervisors are expected to identify the weaknesses of employees; "scientific management," a concept that states clearly that the best way to lead an organization is to keep management separate from workers and follow "scientific" findings to enact the "best" way to stimulate positive outcomes in an organization; "human relations" management that promotes the notion that making employees happy will lead to greater productivity; and "human resource development, in which" it is suggested that employees will feel satisfied if they feel as if their professional goals and objectives are achieved.

The most critical issue considered was not the details concerning the four alternative approaches to management, however. Rather, the issue that was of greatest concern dealt with to ways in which the individual perspectives could be made compatible with what is most critical to an educational leader, namely, ensuring that student needs and interests are addressed and always serve as the defining goal of a good school. In the long run, it makes little difference if an individual school principal is an advocate of human relations or scientific management. What is extremely important is that every leader never lose sight of students as "the center of the circle."

REFERENCES

Daresh, J. C. (2002). *What it means to be a principal.* Thousand Oaks, CA: Corwin Press.

Glickman, C. (1981). *Developmental supervision: Alternative practices for helping teachers improve instruction.* Alexandria, VA: Association for Supervision and Curriculum Development.

Glickman, C. (2003). *Developmental supervision* (4th ed.). Boston: Allyn & Bacon.

Taylor, F. W. (1916). The Principles of scientific management. *Bulletin of the Taylor Society.*

Wilmore, E. (2002). *Principal leadership: Applying the new Educational Leadership Constituent Council (ELCC) Standards.* Thousand Oaks, CA: Corwin Press.

3 Defining Leadership

When Bob Armani was interviewing for his first principalship nearly seven years ago, one of the first questions posed to him by the superintendent of schools, Dr. Rachel Glover, was quite simple. "Mr. Armani, what do you mean by 'leadership'? As you know, the job for which you are applying requires the principal to be a strong instructional leader. I'd like to know what you think all of those words mean to you?"

Bob recalls that he was expecting a question along those lines, but not as quickly as he got it. In preparing for the interview, he thought back over his experience as an assistant principal, coach, and classroom teacher. He even looked over some old notes that he still had around from his days in graduate school at State University. But when he now looked into the eyes of his new potential employer, he realized that the question did not seek textbook or war story kinds of answers. Dr. Glover really wanted to know what the new principal of Joliet Middle School thought his job would be about as a leader. After a few seconds, Bob smiled at the superintendent and said, with an air of confidence, "Leadership is assisting followers to accomplish the goals that we have identified as important to help the children in our school achieve success as learners." That seemed to please Dr. Glover, who jotted down a few notes and moved quickly into another group of questions dealing with more concrete issues such as how he planned to work toward increasing math and reading scores on the state assessment test next spring and how to deal with the likelihood that Joliet might experience a rather large number of new students in the next two to three years as a result of a new housing subdivision that was being built only a few blocks from the campus. None of these issues were unimportant, but neither raising test scores nor handling increased enrollments was an issue that really seemed to get at some basic core beliefs and values such as those touched on by the leadership question.

Even though Bob was now secure in his post at Joliet Middle School and did not plan to look for any other administrative assignments in the foreseeable future, he often reflected on that first question asked by a superintendent who left the district only two years after that interview. In fact, it was the first issue that he tackled each spring when he prepared his "Personal Action Plan" to submit to the assistant superintendent for instruction.

Bob Armani is not alone in his reflection on a central issue faced by everyone who is expected to be a "leader" of an organization. Most individuals do not necessarily hear the question about leadership as the first item in a job interview. But every principal, assistant principal, or educational supervisor faces the issue many times each year, week, or day in the office. Using the title of "Leader" is an easy designation. Actually carrying out the duties the title represents is often a much greater challenge.

This chapter asks you to consider a number of optional ways in which you might define what leadership is all about. No one may ever ask you for a formal definition, but nearly everyone you encounter as a school supervisor or administrator will be looking for signals that you are living the role of leader in a way that is consistent with your own platform. As a result, we will not simply review the great amount of research and literature in education (and in other settings), but rather we will look into the kinds of personalized ways in which you can actually "live" the duties of a leader in your school.

LEADERSHIP FROM A THEORETICAL PERSPECTIVE

As numerous researchers and writers have sought to answer the same question posed to Bob Armani in his job interview, numerous different frameworks have been proposed. In the next few pages, we consider only some selected perspectives that have been developed over the years. These perspectives are organized into two broad classifications of the leadership theories that have been developed. One is "descriptive" theory. Here, the ongoing emphasis is simply on trying to characterize in words the types of things that might be included in the analysis of an important but "slipper" topic. The second set of perspectives deals not so much with definitions and descriptions, but an even more complex issue, namely how to implement leadership behaviors and practices in the most effective ways. This set of perspectives is not limited to "what" questions, but rather the more critical "how" questions of implementing leadership in schools or other settings. These are often described as "normative" leadership theories and analyses. Returning again to Bob Armani and Dr. Glover in the opening scenario, these are the perspectives not addressed in the interview. These represent important issues. After all, had the superintendent pressed Bob for an explanation of "how" he would work with his team in achieving mutually agreed upon goals, the outcome of the selection process might have been very different.

DESCRIPTIVE THEORIES

For years, researchers both in education and in other fields have asked the opening question, "What *is* leadership?" The answers to this question have traditionally been examined through four frameworks:

1. "Great Person" Theories

2. Traitist Theories

3. Situational Perspectives

4. Behavioral Theories

Great Person Theories

A popular way of trying to describe the elusive concept of leadership has been to note that, in the past, there have been many great leaders: Genghis Khan, Jesus Christ, Julius Caesar, Gandhi, Martin Luther King, Jr., Franklin Roosevelt, and many others who are part of written history, and perhaps our personal recollections. Most people know very little about the actual behavior or characteristics of Alexander the Great, but the images of Mother Teresa are still relatively fresh in our minds.

The "Great Person" theories are quite easy to understand. If you want an answer to the question "What is leadership?" all that you need do is think of someone, past or present, who in your own mind represents an image of what you believe to be a leader. Consider this question: Thinking back through recent or even ancient history, who would you think of as people who served as leaders in this world?

_____

_____

_____

_____

_____

_____

_____

Why have you included these individuals on your list?

_____

_____

_____

_____

_____

_____

_____

There is little doubt that there is some value and great appeal to this approach to understanding and describing leadership. After all, most of us grow up with heroes and "great people" who serve as idealized role models in many ways. But there are also great limitations to this approach as well. Most of all, while we may look fondly at the work of one person as representative of "perfect" performance, the fact is that even the most commendable figures are actually far from "perfect" people in many ways. Even more important is the fact that the people we look back on as exemplars were unique to the point that, no matter how hard we try, we will never be able to completely replicate their behaviors and actions. Martin Luther King, Jr., Franklin Roosevelt, and Mother Teresa were truly "one of a kind" people. Still, there is a strong desire for most people to reflect on the virtues of others. After all, consider the number of biographies and autobiographies that reach "best seller" status each year.

If you could identify two or three people (past or present) who you believe are worth emulating as effective leaders, who would they be? Why would you include them on your list?

_____

_____

_____

_____

_____

_____

_____

Traitist Theories

This perspective is somewhat similar to the "Great Person" view because it suggests that a good way to learn about leadership theory is to study the behavior of others as a way to identify specific attributes, characteristics, or traits that are found in effective leaders. The greatest difference in the traitist approach to describing desirable behavior is that there is an effort to look across several different role models and identify the key features that are found in many good leaders so that a listing of generalizable patterns can be made. Thus, if one chooses to look at several famous people perceived to be leaders, it may be possible to note that common ingredients in them might be such things as effective public speaking skills, ability to speak multiple languages, or perhaps common family backgrounds (e.g., having strong positive parental role models, etc.). As a consequence, the inference is drawn that, to be an effective leader, one has to learn how to make speeches, in several languages, while referring fondly to situations where the wise guidance of a mother or father was involved.

If you were to think about several individuals you know, either through reading about them or knowing them in person, what might be some desirable traits that you would notice that were common to everyone on your list?

_____

_____

_____

_____

_____

Quite likely, you noted some things that many associate with characteristics common to leaders. "Intelligence," "visionary quality," "honesty," "winning personality," and many similar attributes are often found in lists of leadership traits. But, what if the people you were thinking of all were one gender, race, socioeconomic status, or had other similar features? Would it not be logical (though not terribly sensible) to conclude that effective leaders might only be male, African Americans, and wealthy? You could also develop lists of successful individuals who only attended Ivy League schools and were over six feet tall. Would that mean that short people who went to the University of Wisconsin could not lead?

There is a tempting tendency for us to try to simplify complex issues such as defining and describing leadership. Traitist Theories of leadership have always been—and no doubt will always be—popular ways of assessing a complex and often elusive concept. But it is always important to note that over reliance on this perspective and others have some definite limitations at times.

There is considerable value in trying to identify concrete examples of how individuals engage in leadership. The "effective schools research" in the early 1980s noted frequently that good schools have good principals who spend most of their time working with their staffs to envision more effective learning. Thus, a trait of leadership that continues as a desirable goal is that of a person being a "visionary." But there is much more to this issue of how to lead organizations.

Situational Theories

Another way of understanding leadership suggests that the specific features of an individual have little to do with a person's ability to lead. Instead, leadership is something that may be independent of an individual; it happens when a particular situation or circumstance requires it of a person. Two very clear examples of this include Audie Murphy, a young Texas high school dropout who looked very "un-leader-like" and "unremarkable" as a farm boy before World War II began, and Rudolph Giuliani, former mayor of New York City. In Murphy's case, he enlisted to serve in the U.S. Army at the beginning of World War II, in part because he viewed it as a patriotic duty, and in part because he saw it as an opportunity to provide him with opportunities for better education and training to help him succeed later in life. Shortly after joining the Army, Murphy was sent as an infantryman to fight in Italy. The demands of combat quickly seemed to draw the young man to higher levels of performance. The relatively unsophisticated Texan quickly became recognized for his qualities of bravery, skills, motivational ability, and loyalty to his comrades. The challenges of combat seemed to draw out every one of these hidden skills from the young man as he repeatedly engaged the enemy, took prisoners, and in many cases, saved the lives of other soldiers. In short, one might argue that a person not likely to ever appear as a leader while he was a poor farmer was unexpectedly thrust onto a stage that called for latent skills to appear suddenly and turn the unknown young man into a leader and national hero. By the end of the war, Audie Murphy became the most decorated and revered soldier to ever serve in the Armed Forces of the United States. He is still seen as a common citizen who became a great leader because circumstances required him to do so.

In the case of Giuliani, he was viewed as a fairly successful mayor of a large American city, but one who had begun to see his potential political fortunes decline due to personal and family issues that seemed to be inhibiting his future success. Although he may have had loftier political ambitions, by the middle of 2001 it was increasingly clear that, like his unsuccessful bid to win election as a U.S. Senator from New York, circumstances may have served as a "ceiling" preventing future goals. Rudolph Giuliani may have simply joined the ranks of dozens of other former big city mayors who never achieved political status beyond municipal management. The horrific events of September 11, 2001 served again as a situation that would change the trajectory of a person from that of "potential leader" to "actual leadership." As most of us would recall the moving images of Mayor Giuliani demonstrating great compassion and love for his fellow New Yorkers after the World Trade Center attacks, his leadership was again made clear not only to his city, but also to Americans and citizens around the world. A situation too horrible to imagine had again served as a shining light on dormant leadership talent. As this book is written, Giuliani seems to be destined to be regarded as a national and even international leader for years to come.

In your own experience, can you recall settings where you or others have had to deal with situations in ways where you "came out of the shadows" to become recognized as a leader?

_____

_____

_____

_____

_____

_____

_____

A major limitation to situational approaches to leadership is that these views suggest that leadership will not likely occur unless the time is right for it to happen. In some ways there is a strong hint that leaders arriving on the scene is based solely on luck. We recognize, however, that the issues facing schools and society in general are becoming much too complex and the stakes are too high for us to simply hope that, because of unpredicted events, people will mysteriously or magically appear out of nowhere. Problems and issues facing American public education appear so frequently and unpredictably that it is not likely to be a successful strategy to sit by and hope that, when things become bad enough, people like Audie Murphy or Rudolph Giuliani will suddenly appear to lead us to victory. In short, situational leadership depends too much on blind luck at times, and education cannot be based on that alone.

Behavioral Theories

As is often the case, perspectives based on only one of two different points of view yield ultimately to compromise. The Great Person Theories and Traitist Theories of leadership took the basic view that characteristics of the individual were the sole determinants of whether a person would be a leader or not. Acting like Abraham Lincoln created leaders, as did demonstrating such attributes as effective communication skills, intelligence, or good interpersonal skills. On the other hand, Situational Leadership tends to state that the individual is not nearly as important as uncontrollable events that put average people into settings where potential leadership is drawn to the surface. In the case of Martin Luther King, Jr., he would not be recognized today as a leader or hero had he come along at a time other than the period of turmoil and strife associated with the Civil Rights campaigns of the 1950s and 1960s.

Behavioral Theories represent a kind of blend of looking at leadership simply as an individual characteristic and as elicited by the circumstances in which a person might find him- or herself. It may be true that the September 11 attack may have evoked leadership on the part of Rudolph Giuliani, but here had to be some internal capabilities of the mayor that enabled him to face the challenge. By the same token, General Dwight Eisenhower may have possessed key characteristics of leadership as a boy growing up in Kansas, but military service and World War II certainly served as a way to ensure that his attributes were noticed. In simple terms, leadership requires a person who can lead by interacting with circumstances that require leadership. If there is a single perspective of leadership that has been most influential in recent years, it is this notion of balance between inherent ability and opportunity. Some recent definitions of leadership that suggest the behavioral approach include:

- Leadership is "interpersonal influence, exercised in a situation and directed, through the communication process, toward the attainment of a specified goal or goals" (Tannenbaum, Weshler, & Massarik, 1961, p. 24)
- Leadership is the "initiation and maintenance of structure or expectation and interaction" (Stogdill, 1974, p. 41)
- Leadership is "a particular type of power relationship characterized by a group member's perceptions that another group member has the right to prescribe behavior patterns for the former regarding his activity as a group member" (Janada, 1960, p. 358)

These and many similar views of leadership offered by Hemphill and Coons (1957), Katz and Kahn (1978), and Patterson (1993) not only emphasize the nature of interaction between the person and the situation or organizational environment, but they also suggest another important part of behavioral leadership theory. That is, leadership must be viewed as a social process, where the dynamics of leader and followers is also a critical issue.

After having reviewed this information regarding the nature of leadership as a social and dynamic activity, how would you assess the value of behavioral theories of leadership as a useful view to those who work in schools?

Many school leaders have noted that any vision of effective leadership must be sensitive to the fact that those who administer schools do not simply lead in isolation. The activities of principals, for example, must be understood in relationship to the groups of those with whom they work each day. In concrete terms, this would explain why it often occurs that candidates for principalships or superintendencies often appear at first to be excellent candidates for leadership positions. They display the attributes of intelligence, good communication skills, and the ability to articulate a vision. But once hired, they cannot seem to do the job. In many cases, it may be that the perceived skills disappear when the reality of the workplace is present.

Many other theorists have been associated with behavioral approaches to leadership. For example, Andrew Halpin and B. J. Winer (1957) noted that the balance of effective leadership is found in two dimensions:

1. *Initiating Structure:* Behavior that delineates the relationship between the leader and members of the work group and endeavors to establish well-defined patterns of organization, channels of communication, and methods of procedure.

2. *Consideration:* Behavior that indicates friendship, mutual trust, respect, and warmth in the relationship between the leader and the staff (Halpin, 1957).

More recently, Stephen Covey (1991) also identified characteristics of "principle-centered leaders" as they engage in behaviors interrelated to organizational environments:

1. *Leaders are continually learning.* Principle-centered leaders are constantly learning from their environments and experiences.

2. *Leaders are service-oriented.* They view their role as providing for the needs of followers.

3. *Leaders radiate positive energy.* They are happy and enthusiastic people.

4. *They believe in other people.* They endeavor to find the best in others, not the fault of others.

5. *They lead balanced lives.* Principle-centered leaders are not "married to their work"; they enjoy a full range of social, intellectual, familial, and work-related experiences.

6. *Leaders see life as an adventure.* They see things that occur in their lives as challenges, not problems.

7. *They are synergistic.* Leaders are able to pull together the vast resources of talent and energy found in people and events that surround them so that they can make organizational life more productive, as the sum of many individual parts.

8. *Leaders exercise for self-renewal.* They engage in regular exercise to strengthen themselves physically, mentally, emotionally, and spiritually.

After having read the various descriptions of leadership offered here, how would you personally describe educational leadership? Which of the four approaches (Great Person, Traitist, Situational, or Behavioral) is most consistent with your own views?

_____

_____

_____

_____

_____

_____

_____

NORMATIVE APPROACHES

In recent years, there has been an effort not only to describe leadership but also to explain the best ways for leaders to behave. These approaches to the analysis of leadership are often referred to as "normative" theories or approaches because they not only attempt to answer the "what" questions but also suggest answers to "how." In the following pages, a few normative perspectives on leadership are presented to enable you to identify more precisely your own personal vision of leadership.

Leadership Grid

The Leadership Grid model of Blake and McCanse (1991) suggests that leadership consists of two attitudinal dimensions: a concern for people, or interpersonal relationships, and a concern for tasks, production, or things.

In this way, there is some overlap with the work of Halpin and Winer (1957) that was reviewed earlier.

The Leadership Grid allows the analysis of leadership, in terms of both concern for people and concern for production, on a continuum of 1 (low) to 9 (high). This model goes beyond simply providing more terms to describe leadership. Rather, its implications about relative effectiveness of behaviors provide useful directions for any individual seeking to perform as an effective educational leader. A Grid rating of 1,1 (the lowest possible levels of both concern for people and concern for production) would hardly be an appropriate pattern for a leader called upon to provide direction to a school staff. A 9,9 rating (the highest possible rating for both concern for people and concern for productivity) would be optimal. Variations on these two complete opposite patterns are likely, of course. A supervisor who truly believes in the value of human relations leadership might be scored as 1,9 (low concern for production, high concern for people) while a 9,1 might indicate high concern for production with low concern for people.

Using the ratings of relative high concern for people and high concern for production derived from Blake and McCanse's work on the Leadership Grid, how do you think you would probably score on these two dimensions? Is this consistent with your sense of how you personally value focus on people as well as focus on production?

_____

_____

_____

_____

_____

_____

_____

Instructional Leadership

For more than a quarter of a century, simply talking about the need for effective leadership in schools has not been seen as a sufficient approach to understanding leader behavior. Instead, "leadership" has increasingly been identified as important in schools only if it fits the normative standard of being something called "instructional leadership." Researchers who studied what characteristics were displayed more often in schools classified as "good" noted time and again that schools which demonstrated the highest rates of student achievement had as a common feature principals who focused their time, talent, and attention on matters associated with instructional improvement.

The Association of Supervision and Curriculum Development (ASCD) (1989) looked at the behavior of many principals who were identified as strong instructional leaders and noted the following five characteristics:

1. *Instructional leaders provide a sense of vision for their schools.* They demonstrate the ability to articulate what a school is supposed to do, particularly in terms of what it should do to benefit children. Effective instructional leaders leave little doubt that the purpose of the school is to find ways in which children may learn successfully.

2. *Instructional leaders engage in participative management.* They encourage a better organizational climate in the school by allowing teachers and staff to participate meaningfully in making decisions of substance, and not merely in an effort to "play at" the appearance of promoting involvement when decisions are already made. The staff senses greater ownership in the priorities and programs that are available to help children.

3. *They provide support for instruction.* Instructional leaders are so committed to maintaining quality instruction as their primary organizational focus that when decisions must be made concerning priorities, instruction always comes first. These individuals make it clear that energy will be expended to assure resources are available to enable the instructional program of the school to proceed unabated.

4. *Instructional leaders monitor instruction.* They know what is going in the classrooms of their schools. This monitoring may take several forms from direct, in-class intensive observation to merely walking around the building and talking with students. The critical issue, regardless of the particular procedures followed, is that instructional leaders are aware of the quality of instruction being carried out in their schools.

5. *They are resourceful.* Instructional leaders rarely allow circumstances in their organizations to get in the way of their vision of quality educational programs. As a result, they tend not to allow a lack of resources, or apparently prohibitive district policies, or any other factors from interfering with the goals of their schools.

How would you assess your personal ability to engage in each of the instructional leadership behaviors?

_____

_____

_____

_____

_____

_____

_____

Other contributors to the field of leadership, Warren Bennis and Burt Nanus (1985), have also studied the behaviors of leaders in many successful organizations and have identified a set of strategies that they believe can be followed by others:

Strategy I: Attention through Vision. Leaders create a focus in an organization, or an agenda that demonstrates an unparalleled concern for outcomes, products, or results.

Strategy II: Meaning through Communication. Effective communication is inseparable for effective leadership.

Strategy III: Trust through Posturing. Leaders must be trusted in order to be effective; we trust people who are predictable and whose positions are known. Leaders who are trusted make themselves known and make their positions clear.

Strategy IV: The Deployment of Self through Positive Self-Regard. Leaders have positive self-images, have self-regard that is not self-centered, and know their worth. In general, they are confident without being cocky.

Strategy V: The Deployment of Self through the "Wallenda Factor." Before his death, the famous aerialist Karl Wallenda was said to have become more preoccupied with not falling than with succeeding. Leaders are able consistently to focus their energies on success rather than on simply avoiding failure.

Have you seen examples of leaders in your own experience that demonstrate one or more of these characteristics of successful performance identified by Bennis and Nanus? What did you learn from them?

_____

_____

_____

_____

_____

_____

_____

BUILDING YOUR PLATFORM

Now that we have reviewed a brief sample of the literature on leaders and leadership, it is time to relate this material to your personal educational platform. What is your personal definition of leadership?

_____

_____

_____

_____

_____

_____

_____

How does this definition relate to your vision of the kinds of things that you believe are critical responsibilities for effective school supervisors or administrators?

_____

_____

_____

_____

_____

_____

_____

KEEPING STUDENTS AT THE CENTER

Remember that the driving purpose of this book is to help you develop a vision of practice that will enable you to continue to maintain the importance of schools maintaining student needs as the center of their work. In your judgment, list three or four ways in which effective school leaders engage in behavior that is clearly related to keeping kids as the target of all that goes on in their schools.

_____

_____

_____

_____

_____

_____

Effective school leaders engage in practices that make it clear that they are leaders of children rather than leaders of school buildings. Regardless of any other time commitments or limitations, people who truly lead through commitment to students provide consistent examples of leading by serving students. They take time to listen. They know names. Above all, they demonstrate respect for students—even when students seemingly do not return respect to others. Regardless of the theoretical model you may select in responding to the question that begins this chapter, it is critical to recall that the greatest thing that most leaders provide to their organization is not simply action. More often than not, what a person models through daily behavior may be the most significant leader action that can be seen each day.

IN REVIEW

This chapter provided information about the various ways in which leadership has been defined and described over the years as a way to assist you in refining yet another plank in your educational platform. Often, words such as "leadership" are used as if there is a widespread agreement as to the meaning of the term. The fact is, there are probably as many different perspectives on what it means to be a leader as there are people who would expect to be identified by this term.

If you are to be an effective leader, it is critical to develop a very personalized understanding of what you plan to do in order to have a positive impact on your school. After all, if the leader does not focus on the centrality of student needs, who will?

REFERENCES

Association for Supervision and Curriculum Development (1989). *Instructional leadership* (Videotape). Alexandria, VA: Author.

Bennis, W., & Nanus, B. (1985). *Leaders: The strategies for taking charge.* New York: Harper and Row.

Blake, R. R., & McCanse, A. A. (1991). *Leadership dilemmas—Grid solutions.* Houston: Gulf Publishing.

Covey, S. R. (1991). *Principle-centered leadership.* New York: Simon & Schuster.

Halpin, A. W. (1957). A paradigm for research on administrative behavior. In R. F. Campbell & R. T. Gregg (Eds.), *Administrative behavior in education.* Chicago: University of Chicago, Midwest Administrative Center.

Halpin, A. W., & Winer, B. J. (1957). A factorial study of the leader behavior description questionnaire. In R. M. Stogdill & A. E. Coons (Eds.), *Leader behavior: Its description and measurement* (Research Monograph Series No. 88). Columbus: The Ohio State University, Bureau of Business Research.

Hemphill, J. K., & Coons, A. E. (1957). Development of the leader behavior description questionnaire. In R. M. Stogdill & A. E. Coons (Eds.), *Leader behavior: Its description and measurement* (Research Monograph Series No. 88). Columbus: The Ohio State University, Bureau of Business Research.

Janada, K. F. (1960). Toward the explication of the concept of leadership in terms of the concept of power. *Human Relations, 13,* 345–363.

Katz, D., & Kahn, R. L. (1978). *The social psychology of organizations* (2nd ed.) New York: Wiley.

Patterson, J. L. (1993). *Leadership for tomorrow's schools.* Alexandria, VA: Association for Supervision and Curriculum Development.

Stogdill, R. M. (1974). *Handbook of leadership: A survey of theory and research.* New York: The Free Press.

Tannenbaum, R., Weshler, I. R., Massarik, F. (1961). *Leadership and organizations.* New York: McGraw-Hill.

4 Deciphering What It Means to "Be in Charge"

M aria Carson had been an assistant principal for nine years in the Eagle Valley local schools before she received word that she was now to serve as the new principal of Eagle Middle School. She was quite confident that her years as an administrator, preceded by seven years as a classroom teacher, would give her the knowledge and skills needed to be successful in her new role. She also knew that, with a very competent assistant principal like Malcolm Connelly, she would do well in her new job.

As her first year at Eagle continued, however, Maria began to have some concerns about the new world of the principalship. Things had started out calmly enough. After all, she had been a school administrator for several years, so she understood a lot about the duties and activities associated with starting a new school year. She was prepared for the usual "ceremonies" of teacher inservice before the first day of class glitches with student schedules, and many other predictable events.

What was becoming increasingly a new reality for the first year principal was something that went well beyond simply knowing a lot of the "how to's" of school administration. She was quite well prepared and experienced in the technical side of being a school principal. But soon after the beginning of the school year, she began to appreciate that there were many things that she did not get involved with as an assistant. Instead, much of what she was now encountering were things that her principal last year had faced without really sharing with Maria.

For one thing, she now realized that there were many times when the principal had to be fairly direct with some members of the teaching staff who did not seem to wish to be able to comply with procedures in the school. She noted, for example, that in a few cases, teachers came to work wearing clothing that did not conform to the "teacher professional dress code" that had been passed by the school board last May. In another case or two, teachers who came late to work needed to be reminded of the contract "report time." None of these were major events. In fact, it was rarely even discernible to anyone but the principal and an individual teacher.

Maria also began to notice the number of times when teachers came to her to gain information, advice, or permission to do certain things. Many were fairly routine matters, but teachers still came to her.

Toward the end of the first semester, Maria had yet another major awakening regarding the realities of her new job. In mid-December, she knew that she would need to reassign three of her teachers. In two cases, the number of students who had withdrawn from Eagle had made it possible to close classes. While some teachers would experience slight enrollment increases in their classes, it was now necessary to transfer the two "surplus" teachers to other district schools that were experiencing significant increases. The other teacher would stay at Eagle, but Maria needed him to be reassigned to teach math classes for students who had failed Algebra in the first semester. In the case of the transfers, Maria had really no choice; she was directed by the superintendent and district personnel director to identify teachers whose teaching loads could be shifted to others in her building so that needed instructional staff could be provided to other district schools. Whether Maria personally wanted to do so or not was irrelevant. What she now began to understand more clearly each day was that, as the principal, she was now responsible for making decisions that were not popular, or easy to carry out. She knew that, even in cases where other teachers were not involved, moving three staff members would be met with a great deal of unhappiness and even anger by teachers. Maria had seen similar situations facing the principals with whom she served as assistant in the past. Now it was her turn to deal with a more unpleasant aspect of her job.

Maria's first year as a principal was actually quite successful. As students left the school at the end of May and teachers completed their work in early June, she had a positive feeling about her work. Parents were happy, students seemed to have had a positive experience, test grades on the state exam were up from previous years, and even teachers who were upset with the mid-year transfer of three of their colleagues seemed to have forgiven "the boss" by the end of the school year. Nevertheless, Maria still felt really drained. She enjoyed the bulk of her work and she was truly happy about her choice of career path. However, despite sitting right next to the principal for a few years, she never had felt the intense pressure of the "hot seat" until now. She was ready for the school year to end so that she could collect her thoughts and get ready for Year Two.

✦✦✦

The principalship is a tough job. Most people who move into that role, whether from an assistant principalship, a counselor's job, or straight from the classroom, know that there are many demands on those who are the official "campus leader." People are generally aware of long hours, demands from parents, high expectations from central office, and occasional conflicts with classroom teachers and other members of staff. Most can see the apparent stress that accompanies administrative jobs. But what people typically do not understand from a distance is that principals often have even greater frustrations that are derived from their status as "the leaders of their schools."

This chapter looks at some of the issues that face both new and experienced principals and how these issues are likely to have an effect on their ability to achieve success in their efforts to focus on the needs of individual students. While there are many different "realities" of leadership that are often faced by people at the beginning of their administrative careers, the discussion here will focus on concerns often expressed by newly appointed administrators, many of whom have had a great amount of experience in schools. These concerns deal with three major realities of leadership: power, control, and authority.

REALITIES OF LEADERSHIP: POWER

Many times, people who are contemplating a shift in their educational careers from the classroom to the administrator's office have some perceptions of the worst part of becoming managers and supervisors. Often, people have a sense that they are not interested in going into administration because administrators are "power hungry" or "control freaks." They simply indicate that the idea of "being in charge," or serving as an authority figure with power, or the requirement to control behavior by others, is not appealing. In the words of one graduate student recently questioned about this disdain for being a boss, "I didn't get into education to push people around."

"Pushing people around" while you engage in a power trip is not a requirement of administrators, whether they work in schools or private corporations. Are there examples of situations where school principals (and hospital executives, branch managers of banks, and CEOs of Fortune

500 companies) engage in improper approaches to the use of their authority? Of course. But the words "power, authority, and control" do not automatically suggest improper behavior. They are normal and regular parts of everyday life for those who serve as managers.

In your own words, how do you react to the concepts of power, authority, and control? Do you have negative reactions to the notion that, as a school supervisor, you will have access to these?

_____

_____

_____

_____

_____

_____

Under what circumstances do you believe it is necessary for a leader to take a very strong approach to the use of power? Give some examples of where this might be a required approach in the administration of a school.

_____

_____

_____

_____

_____

_____

Having power is not just a feature of being an administrator or supervisor. Everyone has power, or at least the potential for exercising power. In simple terms, the German sociologist Max Weber (1947) defined power as "the probability that one actor within a social relationship will be in a position to carry out his own will despite resistance" (p. 52). In this way, power can be understood as the ability of one person to command some degree of compliance on the part of another. Each of us has the ability to encourage another person to behave in some particular way. Even a person whose societal role seems most unimportant may effect some change in others or in society in general.

Reflecting on your behaviors during the past two or three days, indicate some of the ways in which you exercised power (i.e., through control of other people's behaviors).

_____

_____

_____

_____

_____

_____

_____

If you are a classroom teacher, you probably had several immediately obvious examples to describe. You no doubt controlled the behavior of students in many ways, by asking them to be quiet during a class, or not permitting them to leave before the end of a class period, or even by asking them to raise their hands before asking a question in class. If you are a parent, you may think of how you asked your child to be home at a certain time, or to finish homework before watching television, or a hundred other things that parents typically request of their children. As a shopper in a supermarket, you may have reached in front of another shopper to take an item from the shelf, thus causing the other person to seek an alternative. The point is, we all use our power to alter behavior every day. Obviously, many of the examples cited here may be rather small and seemingly inconsequential. Taking one bunch of bananas rather than another will not have significant consequences for very long. But the same can be said of the "controlling actions" of those in administrative roles.

Teachers often complain that their principals and assistant principals frustrate their efforts to work with students by mandating too many rules and regulations. "The principal is on a power trip" is not an uncommon complaint when teachers get together to share stories about life in a school. Some of the "power trip" indicators that have been listed by teachers over the years include such matters as . . .

- walking around the school throughout the day
- requiring teachers to stay out in the hallways during class changes
- insisting that teachers attend evening parent conferences
- demanding the teachers attend inservice sessions
- collecting and reviewing daily or weekly lesson plans
- checking that teachers arrive on time and do not leave early
- ensuring that teachers and staff adhere to all district and school policies
- stopping in to a classroom unannounced to observe a class

What are some other actions of school administrators that might be added to this list of indicators that a leader wishes to exert too much power?

_____

_____

_____

_____

_____

_____

_____

Many who look at the above list might shrug their shoulders and say that the activities noted are only normal events in the life of a typical school. Principals walk around their schools, observe what teachers are doing, check that people are doing their jobs, and so forth. Some have used these kinds of behaviors as indications that the principal is engaged in micromanagement. The interpretation of many activities as examples of intrusive administrative behavior, such as "unannounced classroom visits," might be either unwarranted snooping or, in the eyes of some, a welcome sight which indicates that the principal wants to know what good things are happening in his or her school each day.

Often, it is more important to look beyond outward behaviors to determine if examples of certain practices might be interpreted as "correct" uses of power, or "bad" uses. French and Raven (1960) identified five different sources of social power. As each of these sources is defined, consider the ways in which it may be more or less appropriate as a way to encourage people in a school to achieve agreed upon goals.

1. *Reward power*: the capacity to provide rewards to others in the organization as a way to influence behavior. For example, a school board might offer bonus pay to teachers who perform at a level consistent with established district goals. Administrators and supervisors often exercise reward power in more subtle ways than simply providing extra pay for meritorious service. Some teachers might get better classrooms in better parts of a school, or some teacher might get opportunities for professional development activities more frequently than others.

As a classroom teacher, in what ways have you made use of reward power to promote more desirable student behavior and other educational outcomes?

_____

_____

_____

_____

_____

_____

In what ways have you observed school administrators making use of reward power when working with teachers and staff?

In your judgment, how effective has this type of power been in terms of promoting the attainment of school goals, and also a vision that puts learners "at the center of the circle"?

_____

_____

_____

_____

_____

_____

_____

2. *Coercive power:* the capacity of one person to provide punishment or negative consequences to another in a deliberate attempt to control the other person's behavior. Administrative personnel make use of coercive strategies when they do such things as write negative evaluations of teacher performance or reject new curricular programs that may be desired by some teachers.

In what ways do you or other teachers make use of coercive power with students? In what cases might this be a reasonable approach to using power?

_____

_____

_____

_____

_____

_____

Under what circumstances might it be appropriate for an administrator or supervisor to make use of coercive power to ensure that the school keeps its focus on student needs?

_____

_____

_____

_____

_____

_____

_____

3. *Legitimate power*: Here, control of one person by another is based on the assumption that the person exercising the power has a legitimate right to do so and is supported by a statement of policy, law, or even historical precedent and tradition.

Much of the basis for the power that administrators use "comes with the turf." The licensing agencies that grant credentials to individuals who will serve as school principals or as other administrators give statutory rights and responsibilities to people to exert power and control. When a school district employees a person to "run a school," that person has a great deal of legitimate power. At the same time, a lot of responsibility comes along with that power.

Teachers also have a great deal of legitimate power. Provide some examples of specific cases where teachers have been certified to use this type of power.

_____

_____

_____

_____

_____

_____

_____

Now, indicate some situations where you have noted that school administrators and supervisors are expected to make use of legitimate power in the performance of their duties.

_____

_____

_____

_____

_____

_____

_____

4. *Referent power:* the tendency of other individuals to be attracted by and to identify closely with the person who exercises the power. This is power derived largely from the extent to which people like or respect the person in charge.

As a teacher, have you experienced situations where you believe that some students follow you simply because they like you? What are some of these cases?

_____

_____

_____

_____

_____

_____

Indicate some situations where you have noted administrators or school supervisors who are able to make effective use of referent power.

Under what circumstances does this type of power seem to be most effective?

_____

_____

_____

_____

_____

_____

_____

5. *Expert power*: The ability to influence others' behavior based on special knowledge. This is said to be one of the forms of power most frequently associated with school administration.

What are some examples of the ways in which teachers regularly make use of their special expertise and knowledge as a way to exert power in their classrooms?

_____

_____

_____

_____

_____

_____

_____

Provide some examples of the ways in which school administrators make use of expert power as they lead their staffs in addressing the needs of all students.

_____

_____

_____

_____

_____

_____

These descriptions of alternative sources of organizational power identified by French and Raven provide important insights into the ways in which an educational supervisor or administrator can understand the implications to be derived from reliance on one source or another. Understanding the differences that exist between referent power and reward power, for example, and the likely effect that each is likely to have on people who work in organizations is a powerful guide to behavior. Consider the probable response to an administrator who works at increasing his or her expert powers by learning more about a particular topic as contrasted with the probable response to an administrator who tries to "pull rank" by using threats, punishments, or other efforts associated with coercive power strategies. To be sure, there are times when you will need to rely on some forms of power that may not immediately appeal to you. But the question must ultimately be whether the form of power used is appropriate for the outcome that you need to achieve.

REALITIES OF LEADERSHIP: AUTHORITY

Another unavoidable aspect of serving as the "boss" is that, in that role, you will have authority. The most important question to ponder as you think about this dimension of the world of leadership is simply, "What ways will you use your authority as a school administrator to help your school achieve the central goal of keeping an ongoing focus on student needs and learning?"

Max Weber, the German sociologist mentioned earlier regarding definitions of power, noted the following three major types of authority that are often used in different organizations.

Traditional Authority

In authority derived from tradition, people accept the control of others because it is assumed that those "others" have some sort of traditionally legitimate, absolute right to exercise that authority with no challenge. In schools, for instance, a parent may tell a child to obey a teacher for the simple reason that the person is a teacher, and a teacher always deserves respect. Although this may not be seen in classrooms every day, traditional authority is still widely seen in schools.

Charismatic Authority

This is authority based on the assumption that the leader has some special gift, or even supernatural powers. Examples of this type of authority are religious leaders and some televangelists who, despite apparent inconsistencies in their personal lives, continue to attract millions of followers and their money because the leaders have successfully established in the minds of their adherents that they possess special gifts from God.

Legal Authority

Legal authority is derived from laws, policies, or statutes. Military officers have authority because such authority is decreed by regulation. As many enlisted personnel recognize, superior officers may lack identifiable skills or charisma, but they are in charge simply because they are officers.

Provide one or two examples of how you have seen each of these types of authority in schools in which you have worked.

In addition to considering each of the above types of authority, it may be important to consider the difference between "formal" and "functional" authority. Robert Peabody (1962) defined "formal" authority as authority derived from sources such as the organizational hierarchy, laws, and a person's position in the organizations or office. "Functional" authority comes from such things as a person's professional expertise and competence, interpersonal skills, and suggestion of great experience in handling a particular situation. The tendency to assume that functional authority is "softer" or "better" is really unwarranted. People who exercise authority make use of both approaches. On the other hand, you may deliberately select one particular strategy to achieve a desired goal. A principal who might normally rely on his or her formal authority to bring about changes in the behavior of the teaching staff might choose instead to seek a more indirect way to influence changes in behavior. In other words, the principal might consciously seek to exercise functional rather than—or in addition to—formal authority.

Power and authority are central component elements of the world of administration or supervision. Thus, determining your personal stance regarding these issues is a critical part of defining your own personal administrative platform.

Supervisors and administrators can, in fact, be very effective, and they can be effective without any formal authority. Supervisory effectiveness can rest in functional authority and power. If you learn to engage primarily in behaviors that influence others, then you will be able to bring about change. In school settings, the adoption of techniques designed to have an impact on expertise, competence, and interpersonal skills will probably result in longer-lasting change on the part of teachers and other staff members who are well educated, sophisticated, and accustomed to performing in settings where they must think for themselves. Relying solely on formal authority and "pulling rank" to try to make others perform in a particular way will rarely be effective and will often do more harm than good. Teachers who are told what to do will often rebel against what they perceive as an effort to manipulate their behavior.

The critical issue here is that the responsibilities of being a school supervisor or administrator are intertwined with the concepts of power and authority. What you must decide is the ways in which you will exercise power and authority in a way that is most consistent with your personal vision of what it means to be a leader, and in ways that are consistent with your duties to serve the needs of students.

BUILDING YOUR PLATFORM

After considering the issue of using power and authority in your role of educational leader, you need to consider how this will relate to your educational platform. What do you mean by "being in charge"?

_____

_____

_____

_____

_____

_____

_____

How do your views regarding power and authority relate to your overall vision of the kinds of things that you believe are part of the way in which you can be an effective supervisor or administrator?

_____

_____

_____

_____

_____

_____

KEEPING STUDENTS AT THE CENTER

Keep in mind that your goal is to find ways to ensure that you will be able to maintain a focus on the needs of students as the center of your work. In your judgment, list some ways in which you can exercise that necessary focus with the realities of power and authority as parts of leadership.

_____

_____

_____

_____

_____

Like all administrators, you will be required to engage in behavior that is indicative of engaging in power and authority. That's what is meant by "being in charge," or "being the boss." You will have authority (whether it is obtained by your own personality, legal mandates, or the will of others). As a result, you will be powerful. The most important issue for you to keep in mind is not "if" you have these avenues to exercise control over others, but more important, how you plan to make use of that opportunity to move others toward important goals.

IN REVIEW

This chapter considered two aspects of your new role as an educational leader that are often problematic for those entering the world of administration and supervision. Whether you like it or not, and regardless of what negative impressions you may have related to them, there are two important words that are central to the work of any leader. These are "power" and "authority." You will have access to both, with or without your desire to possess them. The issue considered here is that, first, power and authority have always been a part of your world as a classroom teacher, and you have developed a way of using these characteristics of your job in a way that is not overwhelming to others. Second, as an administrator or supervisor, your duty will be to use these realities of your role with sufficient restraint to ensure that things get done, while also making certain that they do not becomes ends unto themselves. Simply having the opportunity to make people do things will rarely ensure that the right things get done.

The chapter concluded with asking you to reflect on the ways in which you are able to find personal visions of authority and control that are consistent with your personal educational platform. Finally, the most critical issue is always how your personal definitions and understandings of characteristics of leadership can be related to the primary focus of any good school, namely maintaining a focus on the needs of students above all other priorities.

REFERENCES

French, J. R. P., & Raven, B. (1960). The sources of social power. In D. Cartwright & A. Zander (Eds.), *Group dynamics: Research and theory* (2nd ed.). New York: Harper and Row.

Peabody, R. L. (1962, March). Perceptions of organizational authority: A comparative analysis. *Administrative Science Quarterly, 6* (4), 117–122.

Weber, M. (1947). *The theory of social and economic organization* (T. Parsons, Trans.). Glencoe, IL: The Free Press.

5 Dealing With Conflict Effectively

Steve Rawling looked at the calendar on his desk. It was May 28—ten years exactly since Steve received word that he had been named the principal of Larkin Elementary School. He remembered how happy he had been when he got the call from the Associate Superintendent for Human Resources to let him know that he had been successful in his application for his first principalship. He had five years' service as an assistant principal in another elementary school across the district from Larkin. But now, he was going to be in charge of his own building. He recalled that, immediately after the phone call, he telephoned his wife to let her know that he was on his way toward the career in school administration that he had sought for several years. He also remembered thinking that he would look forward to working with children as an instructional leader, and that he would now be able to really move forward with some ideas he had for a long time regarding some instructional practices that could be used to assist children with diverse interests and abilities in his school. He anticipated that there would be times when he could not please all of teachers or all of the parents of his students. But, in general, he believed that he could have a strong impact on the quality of education for the children of Larkin School.

Since his selection as the Larkin principal, Steve has focused his efforts on supporting his strong belief that all children, regardless of race, ethnicity, socioeconomic status, or mental ability, can learn. He has made that statement literally hundreds of times in front of teachers, students, staff, parents, and community groups. For the most part, he has received high praise from the vast majority of individuals in each of the groups with which he has spoken. And people have not only responded favorably to the message; they have supported the messenger. When it was rumored that Steve was about to be moved by the district administration to another elementary school in the district four years ago, there was an enormous outcry by the PTA, teachers, and the local business community. Ten years of service at a particular campus is unusual, but it is indicative of the bulk of opinions in the Larkin community.

In general, Steve is happy with his situation. At the same time, he privately admits that there are some aspects of the job of being the principal that are beginning to wear him down each day. And he is beginning to think about some options. He has considered asking for a transfer to another school, despite what he knows will be protests from many. He has started to think about throwing his hat in the ring for central office positions that are open, both in his current district as well as some other nearby school systems. And he and his family have also had some quiet discussions about the possibility of his retirement from education all together.

Many things have led to Steve's current frustrations. Lack of money, too much time needed to do the job each day, increased emphases on standardized testing as the apparent sole indicator of school effectiveness, and the continued sense that some kids are still being left out are among the greatest concerns that he acknowledges. But there is also the continual bickering, arguing, and general conflict that he experiences "behind the scenes" so often that is causing him grief. He knew before taking the job as a school administrator that he would "never make everyone happy." Conflict and stress derived from it are big parts of any leadership role. But there are many days when Steve just wished that he would not have to hear about parents complaining about teachers, teachers complaining about students, and then hear that office staff members are complaining to the central office or their union because "the principal is ignoring us."

✦ ✦ ✦

Steve is absolutely right about at least one thing: Administrators are not ever likely to please all constituencies all the time. A great deal of popular management literature has features self-improvement prescriptions for leaders to follow. Among the most frequently offered pieces of advice concerns suggestions for ways in which effective managers might be able to reduce, or even eliminate, conflict from their personal and professional lives. Normally, the books note that time management techniques may help in clearing up conflict-riddled lives.

"Sure fire" cures for management blues are often tempting, but they usually have little value in reality. To be blunt, it is virtually impossible to take on any kind of leadership role—whether in education or in any other field—without facing a good deal of conflict in everyday practice. In fact, the more successful an administrator or supervisor becomes, the more likely it is that she or he will experience more intense, frequent, and visible forms of conflict. Consider the example of Steve Rawling in the opening scenario. If he did not have as clear a view of what the central focus of his school should be, he may not encounter as many individuals who would have opposing points of view and conflict may be reduced significantly. Even for those who are not in formal organizational leadership positions, conflict is simply an unavoidable fact of life.

Some people argue that conflict is not only an inevitable feature of organizational life, but it is also a desirable ingredient in effective, functioning organizations. Life without periodic change is stagnant, and the development of conflict is one way to force necessary change. Leaders are legitimately held responsible not for reducing or eliminating organizational conflict but, rather, for using it to promote institutional improvement and growth.

The issue we will consider here is not to avoid conflict, but rather the ways in which you can minimize negative consequences that are likely to result from the conflict in the first place.

RESULTS OF CONFLICT

If conflict is an inevitable fact of life in organizations, what effects might it have? There may be good or bad consequences of any institutional characteristic, including conflict. When disagreements occur, one of two things can always happen. Lack of consensus may lead to improvement in an organization, largely because communication takes place and compromise or further appreciation of the nature of the conflict may be described as "good." On the other hand, disagreement may result in polarization of viewpoints, the end of communication, and personal animosity among members in the organization. Here, the results of the conflict are clearly "bad." As a leader, your job is to guide the conflicts toward a lower level of hostility and therefore toward a higher probability of serving as positive forces in the organization.

Think about a recent conflict that has occurred in your school. Describe the nature of the conflict, what the opposing points of view were, what the issues were, and so forth.

In your judgment, was this type of situation that ended in something that was "good" or "bad" for the school?

_____

_____

_____

_____

_____

_____

_____

If the conflict that you described was good, what were some of the positive outcomes that were achieved? On the other hand, if it was a bad conflict, what were the negative effects of the conflict?

_____

_____

_____

_____

_____

_____

_____

To try to avoid or eliminate conflict is to sidestep an important responsibility of leadership. The results of such behavior will almost always be negative. For example, think of a school principal who would sit in his or her office all day with the door closed simply as a way to avoid any potential conflict This behavior may be satisfying to the principal who enjoys a less stressful job for a short while. Unfortunately, the same cannot be said for those who are hurt because of the conflict situations outside the office door. And learning opportunities to be derived from the resolution of a conflict are lost. In short, schools which feature closed doors on their principal's office are rarely exciting places. Leaders need not stir up conflict purposely, but running from the conflict will not have any positive effect, either.

SOURCES OF CONFLICT

Conflict in a school or in any organization comes from three sources: within the organization, outside the organization, or from within oneself. All three sources may appear on a regular basis in most schools.

Indicate one or more example of a conflict that comes from within a school with which you are familiar.

_____

_____

_____

_____

_____

_____

_____

Now, describe a conflict that has occurred outside of a school and yet has a great impact within that school.

_____

_____

_____

_____

_____

_____

_____

Effective leaders develop the capacity to remain aware of what is occurring within their organizations so that potential conflicts may be identified in advance whenever possible. Developing sensitivity to potential conflicts both inside and outside the organization does not guarantee the prevention of any future conflicts, but it does ensure that leaders will not be surprised (or frustrated) when something happens. There will never be a school in which every teacher gets along with every other teacher, or is totally satisfied with every administrative decision. When leaders make decisions, they can be certain that someone will disagree with those decisions. Poor leaders are unable to anticipate either the likely source or the potency of the conflict likely to arise after the decision is made. Good leaders have a sense of where the "land mines" are located, not as a way to defuse them all in advance (for that would be impossible), but rather to find a path among them that will cause the least damage.

The ability to analyze the kinds of conflict from within grows with the ability to know more about your own values and beliefs. As you react to the challenge to create an educational platform throughout this book, ask yourself how each issue considered increases your understanding of what things you find to be most important in terms of your ability to lead effectively.

TYPES OF CONFLICT

Lipham, Hoeh, and Rankin (1985) identified four types of conflict that are experienced by most leaders of most organizations: interrole, intrareference group, interreference group, and role-personality. In all probability, each of these four types is experienced by virtually every administrator. Understanding these conflict types should benefit anyone going into a leadership role.

1. *Interrole conflict:* "disagreement between two or more roles simultaneously fulfuilled by one person" (Lipham & Hoeh, 1974, p. 137). The leader feels the effects of trying to "wear too many hats."

Most people feel this type of conflict at some point in their lives. For example, teachers work all day in their schools, but they also have personal lives; they have spouses and children and demands on their time that include "taking the kids to movies," going shopping, fixing things around the house, preparing meals, going to social functions, and so forth. In addition, the same teachers might be pursuing graduate degrees at a local university, and they may have some commitment to local civic or church groups. In short, there are many times in the busy lives of people when it is virtually impossible to do all that must be done, and this causes frustration and a sense of failure or at least inadequacy in some people.

What are some examples of the situations in which you feel as if you are "wearing too many hats"?

_____

_____

_____

_____

_____

_____

What steps do you take to reduce this sense of interrole conflict in your life?

_____

_____

_____

_____

_____

_____

2. *Intrareference group conflict:* In this type of conflict, a person is "caught in the crossfire" of different perceptions held by two different factions of the same reference group. The principal is viewed differently by one group of teachers in the school (e.g., the math or science department) than by another group of teachers in the same school (e.g., the English or social studies department).

One academic department (or grade level of teachers) might believe that the principal is not doing enough to represent their needs in the district's budget-making process, while another group of teachers might not worry about the budget, but instead believe that the principal is doing a bad job because he or she is doing little to work with the department in the curriculum development process. Or, experienced teachers believe that the job of the principal is to stay out of their way and spend most of her or his time securing addition resources for their work. At the same time, teachers with little experience in schools might believe that the principal should spend the bulk of his or her time helping them in their efforts to get their careers started successfully.

Give some examples of where you have felt as if you were "caught in the crossfire" between two or more different sets of expectations for your job.

_____

_____

_____

_____

_____

_____

How have you resolved the conflict that came about when others had competing ideas of what you should be doing?

_____

_____

_____

_____

_____

_____

3. *Interreference group conflict:* Here, the conflict is over the expectations for performance held by two different reference groups. For example, the principal of school walks a tightrope between the perceptions that the superintendent and central office administration have for what they believe principals should do and the expectations that are held for the same role by the teachers in the schools.

The school board believes that the primary duty of the principals is to ensure that all the students in their schools do well on the state-mandated standardized achievement tests. On the other hand, teachers believe that there are many more important things for the principal to do besides focusing only on performance on state tests. At the same time, parents demand that the principal invest most of his or her energy in developing more personal development programs for students, and in reviewing school safety standards.

What are some examples of situations where you felt as if you were in the middle of numerous groups' perceptions of what you "should be doing"?

_____

_____

_____

_____

_____

_____

_____

How were you able to handle this type of conflict caused by many groups thinking they knew what you should be doing?

_____

_____

_____

_____

_____

_____

_____

4. *Role-personality conflict:* The job does not fit the person. What an individual believed would be the nature of a job is not consistent with the real demands and expectations of the job.

A new teacher who has dreamed of becoming a teacher for the past several years discovers that there is a lot more to do than simply caring about and teaching children. There are many classroom management responsibilities, discipline is critical (and often more difficult to achieve than first assumed), teachers have out-of-class duties that are often not very clearly related to instruction, and so forth. It is understandable that many new teachers are quickly discouraged and begin to think about alternative careers soon after walking into their first schools.

What is an example of a situation where your perceptions and assumptions about the nature of an assignment were not consistent with the realities associated with that assignment?

_____

_____

_____

_____

_____

_____

How could you have found out more about the realities of the assignment that would have alerted you to the likelihood of a disconnect between what you thought you would experience and what the assignment really involved?

_____

_____

_____

_____

_____

_____

_____

In the case of each type of conflict, you probably had many specific suggestions regarding the ways in which it could have been possible to reduce its negative features. For example, many people note that developing a strict practice of managing your time and developing personal priorities could be a way to make interrole conflict less of a problem in your life. The sense of "wearing too many hats" can be made less problematic if you learn to say "no" to some choices. For example, it may not be a wise thing to begin a doctoral program during the first year in which you serve as an assistant principal. Or you may decide that your involvement with a local citizens' action group may have to take a back seat to your new responsibilities as a parent after a new baby arrives in your life.

Intrareference and interreference group conflict is based on something that you cannot control, namely the perceptions of others regarding what you are "supposed" to do. Most of us realize that we cannot absolutely control the actions of others. We also have to keep in mind that we certainly can do nothing to limit what people think. But what can be done to change perceptions is to be open and honest about what we are doing. This in itself is a way to develop a path toward open communication of the type that can go a long way toward helping people know what your job is all about.

In terms of the role-personality conflicts that often arise in our lives, the best way to head off such grief in the future may be to find ways that will provide you with clear insights into the path that you intend to pursue later. If your goal is to go into the field of educational administration, you have a golden opportunity to find out if that job is really what you want before you get there. Talk to administrators in all sorts of different settings. Realize that school administrators rarely have control over where they will work (in wealthy neighborhoods rather than in places where parents may not be a supportive of the school, for example). As a result, you need to think about what it means to be an administrator, not just what it would be like to be the principal of the school that you dream about leading some day. When it is time to do the internship required for certification in most states, make certain that you throw yourself into the role. Do not simply engage in activity that enables you to pile up hours required by a university or the state education agency. Get your hands dirty, lose some sleep, and work as hard as you would if you were really an administrator. This will not guarantee that you will know everything about being an administrator before you reach that step in your career. But it will help you in making an informed decision about what you may wish to do with your life.

In the long run, there is no magic recipe that can be followed so that you will be able to reduce all conflict of the types noted here. There will be many days when you feel as frustrated (or more) as did Steve Rawling at Rankin School. But there is one big tip that may always help you in understanding the inevitable conflicts that you will face. That is to keep reflecting on your personal values through visiting and refining your educational platform frequently. You may not always be able to change commitments in your own life, the perceptions of others, or the job description assigned to your role. But your values and beliefs belong to you. You will ultimately have less serious disruptive conflict if you at least control your own views.

TIPS TO REDUCE CONFLICT

Larry Hughes (1984) suggested the following strategies that you may also wish to consider as you work toward reducing the negative impact of conflict that you will normally experience as an administrator or supervisor in schools:

- *Analyze your job to clarify precisely what it is you are supposed to do in a particular setting.* Formal job descriptions should be viewed as starting points in *determining* what is expected in a school or district.
- *Determine the difference between managing and doing.* Remember that efficiency (doing things well) must be consciously combined with effectiveness (getting the right things done well).
- *Set personal goals and objectives* and develop strategies for achieving them. Define the goals precisely enough so that they may serve to guide continuing behavior.
- *Conduct a personal time audit* as a way to see how you have really been using your time.
- *Avoid interruptions on the job.* Watch out for "drop in visitors" and unwanted telephone calls that divert you from your focus on effective use of available time.
- *Delegate.* Organize yourself, your subordinates, colleagues, and bosses to accomplish necessary work effectively.
- *Plan and conduct effective meetings.* Meetings should serve the needs of the organization and the people who work in it, not be roadblocks

to effective use of time. Consider how meetings might be arranged to reduce conflict.

- *Organize productive communities and task forces.* A primary cause of many forms of conflict is that one person tries to do too many things. Increase effectiveness not only by delegating particular responsibilities to others but also by assigning tasks and projects to well-organized committees. Consider how others in your organization might be enlisted to reduce competing demands.

After reviewing Hughes's list of tips for reducing conflict, identify two or three items that seem to be most important for you to implement as you move toward greater effectiveness and reduction of the negative effects of conflict.

DEVELOPING A STYLE FOR HANDLING CONFLICT

Each person is likely to have a natural way to attempt to deal with conflict that will be an inevitable part of any role in an organization. David Jamison and Kenneth Thomas (1974) developed a conceptual model that suggests that individuals make use of a "favorite" approach to dealing with situations that cause them stress. They note that people tend to react to conflict in settings in one of two basic ways: (1) People deal with conflict assertively, by becoming aggressive about their own needs above those of others; or (2) people tend to deal with conflict cooperatively, by playing down their own needs and trying to satisfy the concerns of others. Neither of these opposite approaches is seen as sufficient for dealing with all conflict at all times. As the Jamison and Thomas model suggests, people may engage in behavior of five different types: avoidance, compromise, collaboration, competitiveness, or accomodation. Robert Owens (1998) defined each of these behavioral types as follows:

- *Avoidance* suggests withdrawal, peaceful coexistence, and indifference. Avoidance can be useful when (a) the conflict probably cannot really be resolved ("learn to live with it"), or (b) the issues are not so important to the parties to require time and resources needed to work things out. Avoidance can be seen as a kind of "cease-fire" in a conflict state.
- *Compromise* suggests "splitting the difference" between assertive and cooperative behavior. Compromise has some commonalities with collaborative problem solving: (a) if the parties are willing to be engaged in the process, (b) there is some move toward collaboration, and (c) the process is basic conciliatory and not in conflict with the

organization's well-being. Compromise does not move toward problem resolution. Rather, it keeps a lid on the problem.

- *Collaboration* suggests that conflicting parties work together to define their problems and then engage in mutual problem solving.
- *Competitiveness* represents a state of absolute assertiveness. It suggests that a person would be completely committed to the satisfaction of personal concerns, without attention to the needs of others.
- *Accommodation* is complete submission of one's personal interests in favor of efforts to satisfy the needs of others. It is often seen as complete acquiescence to the will of others in matters of conflict.

How would you assess your personal tendency to relate to one or more of the above behavioral types when faced with the need to react to conflict in your personal or professional lives? (For example, do you tend to try to "find a middle ground"(compromise) typically faced with conflict? Or would you prefer to simply ignore conflicts (avoidance)?

_____

_____

_____

_____

_____

_____

_____

REALITY OF CONFLICT

As noted earlier, "you can't make everyone happy all the time." Not many people look forward to the idea that they will need to engage in conflict as an ongoing feature of their job. Few people relish the thought of telling an employee that he or she is fired or a qualified candidate that he or she did not get a desirable job. Some might even say that conflict, though a normal part of organizational life, is still irrational behavior. People find conflict so difficult because they are human beings who constantly strive for rationality.

Administrators and supervisors serve at the crossroads of many competing agendas, value systems, and points of view. Leaders receive directions from others that they must implement. At the same, they work with others—as colleagues, students, employees, and so forth—who must also receive direction. And conflict arises.

Conflict is ultimately avoidable only through total withdrawal from reality. It might be said that death is the only absolute escape from conflict. That, obviously, is not a reasonable choice. The best course that you may need to follow is to accept conflict and realize that the only thing to fear may be allowing conflict to take over your life. The message here should be clear: Learn to live with conflict, but don't let it control behavior.

BUILDING YOUR PLATFORM

The inevitability of conflict being a part of your life as a school leader makes this issue an important plank in your personal educational platform. In the space below, write a description of how you plan to deal with the conflicts that you are undoubtedly going to encounter in your life as a professional administrator or supervisor.

KEEPING STUDENTS AT THE CENTER

It may sound like a contradiction, but one of the greatest sources of conflict in many schools is related to the ways in which it may be possible to meet publicly stated commitments to a principle that should be universally accepted as important by all educators. Simply stated, there are much controversy surrounding the issue of how to maintain and demonstrate a serious commitment to addressing the needs of all students as the central mission of all schools. In recent years, focusing on student needs has increasingly been defined as making certain that there are data to ensure that all children are learning fundamental skills and knowledge at an appropriate level. Thus, we find things like "No Child Left Behind" legislation at the national level, complete with expectations that all teachers are "highly qualified" and that "adequate yearly progress" is being made by all students in all schools. But we also know that, while these measures have become nationwide expectations, they are hardly seen universally as actions that will truly ensure that schools are serving the needs of all students.

Regardless of what controversy or conflict presents itself regarding the proper way of serving students, funding for education, or any other issue that exists regarding what should or should not be taking place in schools, remember that, in the long run, one of the most significant duties of anyone in an educational leadership role must be to make certain that the frustrations we often feel do not impact on the educational program. Simply stated, students cannot become pawns in a game of chess that is played between school personnel and politicians. They cannot become the prize in contests of competing ideologies related to what is the best way to measure student learning. Such dialogue is, of course, important in the broader realm of educational inquiry. But it cannot hamper the ability of third graders to learn how to use mathematics, or high school juniors to learn chemistry.

In your judgment, what are some of the controversies in your school or district that may have a negative impact on the ability of your school to serve student learning needs? How will you manage this type of conflict in your school?

_____

_____

_____

_____

_____

_____

IN REVIEW

Conflict is defined simply as a disagreement between two parties. Conflict becomes more intense with the introduction of additional emotional commitment and hostility. As a result, leaders need to be able to understand

and interpret what is really happening when conflict occurs in their schools. Above all, leaders must be able to assess their own involvement in conflict, whether as the apparent cause of controversy at times, the observer of conflict among others, or the person who takes on the role of peacemaker to resolve conflict situations The key to this type of leadership skill comes from the ability to appreciate such issues as the types of conflict that are involved, and also personal feelings of the most appropriate ways to handle conflict.

Being a school leader requires the demonstration of many skills. Perhaps one of the most important is the ability to model certain behaviors and attitudes. Conflict will always exist in all organizations, but an effective leader will not allow that fact to impair pursuit of the most critical objective, namely student learning.

REFERENCES

Hughes, L. W. (1984). Organizing and managing time. In J. M. Cooper (Ed.), *Developing skills for instructional supervision.* White Plains, NY: Longman.

Jamison, D., & Thomas, K. (1974). Power and conflict in the teacher-student relationship. *Journal of Applied Behavioral Science, 10*(3), 326.

Lipham, J. M., & Hoeh, J. A. (1974). *The principalship: Foundations and functions.* New York: Harper and Row.

Lipham, J. M., Hoeh, J. A., & Rankin, R. (1985). *The principalship: Concepts, cases, and competencies.* White Plains, NY: Longman.

Owens, R. G. (1998). *Organizational behavior in education* (5th ed.). Saddle River, NJ: Prentice Hall.

PART II

Views About the People Who Make Up a School

6 Revisiting Who Teachers Are and What They Do

M ary Badger and James Buckminister had been serving as assistant principals together at Green Cheese High School for the past three years. They had completed their administrator certification programs at State University at the same time, and they were friendly competitors for several administrative positions in school districts around Lake City, the state capital. All of a sudden, they both received callbacks from the principal at Green Cheese. At first, he was looking for only one assistant principal to join him, but due to an unanticipated resignation, he now had two openings. He indicated in his phone calls that he had been impressed by both Mary and James, and he now could hire both of them.

Mary and James were very happy with the calls they received, and they called each other almost immediately. "Suddenly the two competitors have been brought to the 'peace table' together. Should we agree to a truce and give Lake City the 'dynamic duo'?" James was enthusiastic about his willingness to join Mary in "providing the Lake City area with the most outstanding assistant principals in the state."

At their first administrative team meeting, they met with Mike Mendota, the principal, and Marianne Monona, the third assistant principal. After talking about backgrounds and specific goals for the next year, Mike indicated that he planned to follow the same assignments that he had in the past with three assistant principals. Since Marianne was the most experienced, with three years of experience completed at the school, she would begin the year as the assistant principal in charge of curriculum, instruction, and staff development. She had learned a lot from working with senior colleagues for the past few years, and now she would make use of her experience by working on the master schedule, planning most of the teacher inservice for the year, and continuing the curriculum alignment project that had already started at Green Cheese. She would also deal with some student discipline and continue to evaluate teachers in the fine arts programs, physical education, and special education. Since Mary had been an English teacher and James taught chemistry and physics, it was easy to distribute the other evaluation duties. James would work with science and math teachers, while Mary would evaluate the social studies and English teachers. Mike would continue to be primarily responsible for working with the foreign language department and also the seven first year teachers who would be joining the faculty for the fall term. In addition, the two "rookies" would share the bulk of discipline referrals along with the management of the school physical plant and facilities.

The first thing that Mike suggested to all three assistants was to get out in classrooms as soon as possible so that they could get some early insights into the teaching practices of the teachers in their assigned subject areas. It was much too early in the school year to do any formal observations, but it was never too soon to establish visibility in classrooms and rapport with the professional staff.

After that first meeting, James and Mary found a bit of time to get some coffee and talk about their immediate impressions of their new lives as assistant principals in a high school.

"I knew that we would be doing most of the 'grunt work' with discipline. They're not going to give rookies too much to do with the instructional stuff yet. I guess I'm kind of glad about that," Mary started. "But I was a caught a little off guard by the assignment of evaluation duty so quickly. I don't quite know if I'm ready for that yet."

James agreed with his colleague's lack of surprise over getting handed student discipline as a beginning chore for new administrators. But his response concerning the early start of classroom observations was somewhat different from Mary's. "I don't think it's too soon at all. What are you going to learn about these teachers that you don't already know about these folks in the first place? Look, you've been a teacher for as long as I have, and you should pretty well know what to expect out there in the school. There are a lot of the teachers who are just going through the motions. By comparison, you can identify the good ones pretty quickly and then you'll know that the others are really the ones you'll have to keep an eye on throughout the year. There're a lot of bad teachers out there, and our job between dealing with the discipline cases will have to focus on rounding up the really bad teachers so that we can document their incompetence and help the boss get rid of them."

"So you don't think we need to get to know the teachers that well?" Mary asked.

"Why?" responded James. "There are plenty of bad teachers, but the good news is that there are also plenty of applicants to the district for teaching positions here. This district has a great rep and pays the highest salaries in the state. Teachers are teachers are teachers. It's good to shake things up and let some new blood in here—for the kids' sake."

✦ ✦ ✦

School administrators and supervisors no longer spend time as teachers in classrooms, but they have a great deal to do with the oversight of quality educational practice in their schools. The great difference between what teachers can do and what can be done by administrators is that administrators have to rely on their teaching staff to "make things happen." As a result, one of the most important issues for any school leader to consider may be his or her ability to relate effectively to classroom teachers. And the basis of relationships is found in the attitudes that the leader has regarding the teachers. This chapter will ask you to reflect on the nature of who teachers are, what their world is like, and most of all, how you perceive their value in your own professional value system. This should lead you to developing yet another clear understanding of an important plank in your personal educational platform.

Before looking at some of the issues covered in this chapter, let's consider some of the ideas that are covered in the opening scenario. If you had to write a statement that would probably be found in Mary's educational platform regarding her view of teachers, it might be:

_____

_____

_____

_____

_____

_____

What statement could have been written as part of James's platform plank regarding his view of teachers?

_____

_____

_____

_____

_____

_____

_____

WHO ARE TEACHERS?

General characteristics of teachers in the United States might be seen as strong determinants of how others—including school administrators— might view this group in their value statements. To answer this question, it is worthwhile to review some research that has been done over the years. What the data collected in those studies show time and again is that findings regarding the basic features of teachers have remained relatively constant for many years.

First, research has shown that teachers have traditionally come from humble backgrounds. Historically, teachers have been depicted as representatives of the middle class or even lower middle class, but these designations may be somewhat meaningless in present-day society. However, it is clear that the majority of teachers do not come from wealthy backgrounds.

Second, a large number of teachers have normally represented the first generation of college graduates in their families. Some evidence suggests that this factor is changing as more people in society have access to university studies. Nevertheless, while physicians and attorneys often come from families with a long tradition of access to higher education, the same cannot generally be said of classroom teachers. Dan Lortie (1975) suggested that controlled access to a college education is an important common characteristic of teachers and teaching. Socioeconomic constraints typically reduce the range of career choices available to those who eventually become teachers.

Another issue concerns the family backgrounds of most teachers. Those who teach in schools often come from families that cannot be selective when it comes to choosing a college, but this characteristic serves to entice people into teaching in the first place. People who have great difficulty in paying for post-secondary education are still able to look at teaching as a realistic professional goal because teaching is still a professional role that can be achieved with only an undergraduate degree in most states. The extent of the financial outlay required for medical school or law school prevents most people from pursuing those careers.

Research also suggests that teachers select the classroom as a career goal fairly early in their lives. Traditionally, women have tended to identify teaching as a likely career while they were still in elementary school, and men at least tentatively choose teaching by the time they exit high school. More recently, it appears that teachers are beginning to make these career choices a bit later in their lives in part, no doubt, because women now have more options available than they once did. In addition, programs allowing for "alternative teacher certification" routes into the classroom are opening the doors to teaching careers to many who did not consider the world of professional education desirable earlier in their lives.

Profiles of the teaching field in the United States, which have been developed by state departments of education and professional organizations, substantiate other characteristics:

1. *Racial/ethnic characteristics:* Teachers in the United States tend to be white, although the 10 percent of the teachers across the nation who are African American come closer to equaling the nearly 12 percent of the general population that is also African American. Of African American teachers, more are female that male. Greater disparity occurs in terms of the ever increasing Hispanic population, particularly in states not traditionally assumed to have high Hispanic school populations. In addition to states such as California, Texas, Arizona, and Florida, other states, such as New Jersey, Illinois, and Ohio, now have large percentages of school age Hispanic children, but few Latino teachers. Across the United States, demographers (Hodgkinson, 2000) note that by 2020, the U.S. population will be approximately 18 percent Latino, while there will likely continue to be fewer than 10 percent of the nation's teachers who will be Hispanic (Luster & McAdoo, 1994; Odden, 1995).

2. *Gender distributions:* Nearly 60 percent of American teachers are female. In addition, there is a historic tendency for the percentage of male teachers to increase at more advanced levels of schooling (i.e., as one moves from elementary to middle schools to high schools) (Regan & Brooks, 1995).

3. *Age levels and teaching experience:* Although recent shortages of teachers in some areas of the country and in some subject specialties are beginning to have an impact on the average ages and years of experience of teachers in the United States, averages continue to rise. In 1911, the average age of teachers was 24. and the typical teacher had five years of experience in the classroom (Rodgers, 1976). Today, the typical teacher is slightly more than 35 years old, with approximately 11 years' experience. These figures are higher in larger school systems where there is traditionally less turnover among teachers (Cunningham & Cordeiro, 2000).

These characteristics provide us with an interesting snapshot of American teachers. Teachers do not generally come from among the ranks of the wealthy and they often have had to work hard to pay for the education needed to reach their goal—a goal that was typically established early in life. The "typical" teacher is white, female, in her mid-thirties, and married.

Review the characteristics of "typical" classroom teachers noted above and note the ways in which your background and characteristics are consistent with this image.

_____

_____

_____

_____

_____

_____

_____

If one generalization might be made, teachers appear to come from a relatively homogeneous pool of people; they tend to be more similar to, rather than dissimilar from, one another.

WHAT ATTRACTS AND MOTIVATES PEOPLE TO BE TEACHERS?

Before we consider what others have said about the reasons that typically attract people to become classroom teachers, list one or two of the more powerful reasons that have drawn you into the field of professional education.

_____

_____

_____

_____

_____

_____

_____

Compare your reflections with the findings of Dan Lortie (1975) as he interviewed many teachers to determine why they were initially attracted to the teaching profession. He identified five different themes:

1. *The interpersonal theme.* Teachers often say that they pursued their careers because they truly enjoyed working with young people.

2. *The service theme.* Some people select teaching careers because they believe that, by devoting their lives to this work, they can fulfill some special mission insociety.

3. *The continuation theme.* Some individuals become teachers because they were comfortable as students sheltered in the world of schools. As they grew, they continued to be so attached to life in schools that they did not wish to leave that environment.

4. *Material benefits.* Some people select teaching because it provides prestige, money, and employment security. This may be surprising in light of the fact that many are aware that life in the classroom does not make a person rich or socially prominent. However, when one recalls the earlier point that teachers come from modest backgrounds, teaching represents a source of predictable income.

5. *Time compatibility.* An old saying suggests that the best reasons for going into teaching are "June, July, and August." People find teaching appealing because it offers more time for the pursuit of other interests and responsibilities. Parents of young children at home see teaching as a way to earn a steady income while being able to spend nights, weekends, and holiday periods with their families.

Which of the above attractors to teaching are most consistent with factors that influenced you in your career selection?

_____

_____

_____

_____

_____

_____

_____

Are there any additional characteristics of life in classrooms that appealed to you and influenced your career decision making?

_____

_____

_____

_____

_____

_____

_____

Others (Armstrong, Henson, and Savage, 1981) identified more motivating factors to explain why people select teaching as a career choice:

1. *Nice working conditions.* Teachers often note their favorable impressions of both the physical environments in which they work and the kinds of people with whom they work. Teaching is also perceived as a job which provides for considerable autonomy.

2. *Lack of routine.* Teachers describe teaching as a job in which they can avoid the kind of daily monotony that they would find working

in offices or other settings. Students are diverse, and each day in a classroom provides new challenges and experiences.

3. *Importance of teaching.* Some teachers report that they do what they do because they view their work as a way to transmit culture to new generations, provide information to youngsters, serve as positive role models, and achieve many other goals that will benefit society.

4. *Excitement of learning.* Many teachers were good students themselves, and they now continue to believe in the fundamental value of learning.

In addition to the attractors and motivators noted here, what other things may explain why people choose to go into teaching?

_____

_____

_____

_____

_____

_____

_____

Your list may included such things as "significant role modeling" by favorite teachers or by observing relatives (mother, father, aunt, uncle, older siblings) who were successful teachers. Or, there may specific issues that compelled you to choose teaching as a job. Whatever the reasons, however, teachers tend to have many similarities in their backgrounds. And when you go into administration, remember always that the people with whom you work as a leader are not that different from you.

WHAT DO TEACHERS DO?

Simply stated, teachers teach. But they also engage in behaviors and experience conditions that tend to define the reality of teaching as a professional role and life choice. Anne Lieberman and Lynne Miller (1984) studied conditions in teachers' lives that appeared characteristic of all who work in classrooms. This analysis yielded the following list of what the researchers referred to as the "social realities of teaching."

1. *Teaching style is highly personalized.* A contradiction of classroom teaching is that teachers strive to make their contact with students as individualized as possible (keeping student needs in the center), while they are also faced with the reality of working with 25 or more students at a time. This results in teaching practices which are followed because teachers find unique and idiosyncratic ways of dealing with the needs of individuals and groups at the same time.

2. *Teachers' rewards are derived primarily from students.* When students indicate that they have an interest in what is being taught (by studying for exams, doing their homework, participating in class discussions, and so forth), teachers perceive this as an affirmation of their personal worth.

3. *Teachers are uncertain of the link between their teaching and student learning.* Teaching is much like "shooting an arrow in to the air" and never knowing where it may fall. Most teachers feel frustrated by their inability to see the ultimate results of their work.

4. *The knowledge base of teaching is weak.* Teaching, unlike medicine, law, engineering, and other professions, possesses no unified and highly codified body of knowledge that provides clear direction to those who wish to "cover what is important."

5. *The goals of teaching are vague and often conflicting.* What are teachers "supposed" to do? Disseminate a fixed body of knowledge? Entertain? Babysit? Serve as role models? The lack of clarity about a teacher's role leaves many teachers with no true understanding of a single purpose.

6. *Control norms are often seen as necessary features of schools.* Educational goals are not always clear, but the end result usually is: Schools are expected to exercise strong control over young people to guarantee that social order is maintained.

7. *Professional support is lacking.* Although contact between people (i.e., teacher-to-student, student-to-teacher) is a primary feature of teaching, teachers are remarkably isolated as workers, particularly from colleagues and other adults.

8. *Teaching is an art.* Efforts to make teachers conform to behavioral patterns that represent "good teaching" are usually futile because artists struggle to express their uniqueness and resist conformity.

As you consider these "realities" of what it is to be a teacher, which items cause you the greatest concern or difficulty as you work in your classroom each day? To what extent might these features be problematic to you as you work with teachers when you step into the role as an administrator or supervisor?

_____

_____

_____

_____

_____

_____

_____

WHAT DO TEACHERS EXPECT OF LEADERS?

Joseph Blase and Peggy Kirby (1992) carried out a comprehensive review to determine what expectations teachers hold for their principals and other administrators. They noted the following issues:

1. *Teachers seek principals who use praise honestly, openly, and sincerely.* Teachers seek and respect people who will provide them with open, honest, and straightforward comments, and provide praise when it is warranted. They do not seek vacuous platitudes and commendations without substance.

2. *Teachers look to their principals for high expectations regarding professional performance.* Teachers respect most those administrators who have a clear vision of what they want to see accomplished in their schools, and then hold themselves and teachers accountable for achieving that vision.

3. *Teachers want to be involved.* Teachers want to feel as if they are part of the activities in their schools.

4. *Teachers seek professional autonomy.* Teachers believe they are truly professionals who have the expertise in what they teach and how they should teach it. They appreciate leaders who respect that perception.

5. *Teachers want administrators who support them.* Teachers want leaders who provide opportunities for professional development, needed instructional materials, and support in such matters as student discipline and parent confrontations.

6. *Teachers do not want to be told "how to" do their jobs.* Teachers know that they can often improve their performance in certain areas, and leaders can help them. They most respect situations where their principals show them how, or "nudge them" toward different practices.

7. *Teachers respect principals who act in a way that earns respect.* Teachers do not respect administrators who tell them that they must comply with policies simply because they have been told to do so. Instead, they will follow and respect those who engage in the use of authority derived from expertise and ability.

8. *Above all, teachers want principals to be "mirrors to the possible."* Teachers want to do a good job; they want to be challenged to achieve success. Such efforts come about in a climate where everyone is challenged to achieve success. Principals must advocate a clear vision for the school, and teachers will respect leaders who have a vision that goes beyond simple daily survival in their schools.

The picture of what is viewed by teachers as effective leadership by principals and other administrators consists of more than simply repeated calls for high performance on the standardized tests for the year. That is truly a matter of survival in these days of "No Child Left Behind" and high stakes accountability testing. What teachers want to do goes well beyond "getting the numbers up."

What additional characteristics of effective leadership can you add to the list of teachers' perceived effective behaviors and practices for educational leaders?

SO WHAT DOES THIS MEAN TO YOU?

In a job where the ability to engage in productive interpersonal relationships is critical to success, there may be no more important relationships for school administrators and supervisors to cultivate than those with teachers. After all, administrators do not carry out the daily primary duty of any school, namely teaching students. They cannot. Therefore, they must rely on teachers in the schools to engage in the core activity of teaching to promote students' learning. Some have even defined effective school leadership as "teaching teachers." But the administrator impacts on this process very directly in terms of how she or he is able to interact effectively with classroom teachers as a way to ensure that their productivity and success is high. If teachers are not effective, student learning will obviously suffer. And teachers are not likely to be effective without positive interactions with their supervisors.

In most cases, school administrators have had to spend anywhere from three to five years as classroom teachers before they even qualify for an initial license or certificate from the state to serve as an assistant principal or principal. In your opinion, is this a good policy to maintain, or should the doors to the principalship be opened to those who have demonstrated good administrative talent, regardless of whether they have been teachers or not?

_____

_____

_____

_____

_____

_____

The theory behind requiring school administrators to have spent time in classrooms as teachers is that only those who have been teachers can understand how to relate to and work effectively with teachers in schools. In turn, working effectively with and understanding teachers also requires another skill or insight for administrators—empathy for those who instruct children. Therefore, it is not a novel concept to think that administrators have a sense of what he job of teaching involves. However, merely having "walked in the footsteps of others" does not guarantee any particular attitude toward "others." In fact, past experience as a classroom teacher could give a person a perspective that is less than positive about teachers. There are some individuals who choose careers in educational administration because they are frustrated with what they have seen when serving as a teacher: some teachers are not very good, dedicated, caring, competent, and many other attributes. The result is that some people leave the classroom so that they can "straighten things out with all the bad teachers out there." The perceptions of these individuals is that teachers are not to be trusted, believed, or allowed to have a great deal of autonomy in the classroom. In the terms that we considered in Chapter 2, administrative "inspection" might be the prevailing philosophy of some supervisors or administrators because they had been teachers in the past but had bad experiences with their colleagues.

Of course, there are many other ex-teachers who are now administrators who have extremely high regard for classroom teachers because they had spent years getting to know professional educators who were talented, caring, and committed to serving the needs of children.

The point of this review is to note that an administrator's basic assumptions about teachers are a critical determinant of how that leader will be able to work with those who are going to be in contact with children each day. It is not the purpose here to proclaim that a successful administrator must possess only one view of teachers and their roles and abilities. Rather, this is to suggest that an extremely important part of an administrator's personal professional platform must be as reflection on the strengths and weaknesses perceived in teachers in general.

BUILDING YOUR EDUCATIONAL PLATFORM

After reflecting on the backgrounds of teachers, the kinds of things that probably attracted them into the profession, the factors that motivated people to do the job, and other variables associated with "typical teachers," how would you describe your fundamental beliefs and values related to those who work in classrooms with students? For example, do you believe that teachers are highly skilled and dedicated professionals who deserve a great deal of leeway in terms of how and what they teach, or do you believe that teachers are basically to be seen as district employees who work hard, but do not necessarily possess the skills and abilities associated with true professionals?

_____

_____

_____

_____

_____

_____

_____

Based on your basic assumptions regarding teachers, what effect will your value orientation have on your ability to work effectively with teachers in delivering instruction in your school?

_____

_____

_____

_____

_____

_____

It is possible to have many different views of teachers. But the most critical issue that any administrator or leader needs to keep in mind is that, regardless of personal perspectives, teachers have a great deal to do with how well the overall school is able to maintain its commitment to the central vision of ensuring that the needs of students drive the rest of the school's operation.

In light of your personal platform statement regarding the role of classroom teachers, how will these staff members be able to assist in directing the school toward service to all students?

_____

_____

_____

_____

_____

_____

_____

IN REVIEW

This chapter provided you with a great deal of information concerning the background characteristics of teachers in the United States. The purpose of this review was to assist you in making a determination of one of the most critical aspects of your educational platform. How you personally view teachers will have a great impact on the ways in which you are likely to interact with the people who interact with students each day. As we reviewed these characteristics, you were asked to reflect on how these issues are likely to impact on your thinking and valuing regarding class-room teachers. Are they colleagues or simply your employees?

REFERENCES

Armstrong, D. G., Henson, K. T., & Savage, T. V. (1981). *Education: An introduction.* New York: Macmillan.

Blase, J., & Kirby, P. (1992). *Bringing out the best in teachers: What effective principals do.* Thousand Oaks, CA: Corwin Press.

Cunningham, W. G., & Cordeiro, P. A. (2000). *Educational administration: A problem-based approach.* Boston: Allyn & Bacon.

Hodgkinson, H. (2000). *Secondary schools in a new millennium: Demographic certainties, social realities.* Reston, VA: National Association of Secondary School Principals.

Lieberman, A., & Miller, L. (1984). *Teachers, their world, and their work: Implications for school improvement,* Alexandria, VA: Association for Supervision and Curriculum Development.

Lortie, D. C. (1975). *Schoolteacher.* Chicago: University of Chicago Press.

Luster, R., & McAdoo, H. P. (1994). Factors related to the achievement of young African American children. *Child Development, 65,* 1080–1094.

McDonald, J. P. (1992). *Teaching: Making sense of an uncertain craft.* New York: Teachers College Press.

Odden, A. R. (1995). *Educational leadership for America's schools.* New York: McGraw-Hill.

Regan, H. B., & Brooks, G. H. (1995). *Out of women's experience: Creating relational leadership.* Thousand Oaks, CA: Corwin Press.

Rodgers, F. A. (1976). Past and future of teaching: You've come a long way. *Educational Leadership, 34,* 97–99.

7 Exploring the How and Why of Teacher Evaluation

M elissa Ontiveros was extremely happy to get the word that she would be joining the administrative team at Glowing Fire High School, a school where she had been a teacher for the past nine years. When she announced to other faculty members that she had decided to apply for the assistant principal opening at Glowing Fire to her friends on the faculty, they were glad that she had a chance to step in and become one of the three campus administrators. It had been a long time since they had a colleague "from the trenches" serving in an administrative position.

When Melissa met with Mary Cariopolis, the principal, and Winston Salem, the other assistant principal, the group talked about how they would divide their duties this next year. All three agreed to work with student discipline. Winston was already serving as the athletic administrator for the school, and that duty would remain as part of his job description. Melissa would work on staff development and the curriculum. Mary, of course, would continue with her duties as the principal, with particular emphasis on maintaining effective working relationships with parents. And the three administrators would take on staff evaluation duties, with each administrator working primarily with certain subject departments. Since Melissa had been a math teacher, she was now responsible for evaluating teachers in science and math, as well as performing arts. State law and the master contract with the local teachers' association required that each teacher be evaluated formally at least twice each school year, by no later than the first of March. And first and second year teachers were expected to receive three formal evaluations. Melissa had three on her list who would need that extra attention this year. The two assistants were also informed by the principal that this would be the last year in which the current evaluation instrument would be used in the district. At a recent principals' meeting, it was announced that the board and superintendent were now asking that the administrators in the district begin to develop a much stronger set of guidelines to follow in staff evaluation. Several board members were convinced that too many marginal and even poor teachers were "getting through" the current system; things had to be more demanding so that the district would retain its position as a strong, well-respected academic system in the state. The theme of tightening up the evaluation system as a way to "get rid of dead weight" among the district teachers was reinforced by comments made by the superintendent at the first districtwide administrative inservice that Melissa attended three days before the school year started.

A few weeks after the school year began, Melissa's friends in the math department decided to take their old friend out to dinner to see how things were going in her new job. Melissa was happy to have this chance to reconnect with her old group; in a very short time, she had started to feel as if she were getting farther and farther away from her roots in the classroom. Besides, she needed a break from the seeming non-stop work that she had been doing since stepping down the hall to the administrative offices. She liked her new position, but it was extremely time-consuming.

The first math teacher to toast their former colleague was Regina Gilhooly, chair of the math department. "I was sad to have you leave us, but I'm glad to know that the teachers are finally getting a voice in the front office. We've needed someone from inside the building to get an administrative job here for years."

"You can say that again, Regina," said Bob Williams, a teacher who had been at the high school longer than anyone else in the math department. "And this year, it's really critical for us to have a friend in high places. Did you guys read in the paper last month how the superintendent is going along with the new board-inspired 'get the teachers evaluation scheme'?"

"I think they're just trying to get rid of a bunch of us old timers who cost the district too much. We aren't ready to retire, but we can be 'evaluated' out of the school," David Karnofsy, another veteran math teacher noted.

"Actually, I don't think that I have any problems with the idea that they want to change the evaluation process here. As a second year teacher, I can tell you that what I went through last year was a waste of time. I 'passed' with flying colors. I knew I was okay before they even gave me my evaluation results. I also knew there were some areas where I needed to improve, but the evaluation didn't give me any hints in terms of how I could get better this year," observed Tanya Chen.

The dinner concluded, and Melissa went home with more on her mind than she expected after a social event. In only a few weeks, she was planning to do her classroom "walk throughs" to get an informal read of what was happening with her teachers. But now she had suddenly realized that this evaluation business was going to be a lot more difficult than she had realized. The district wanted one thing, some teachers wanted a different spin, and other teachers were looking for other things from the evaluation process.

✦✦✦

Evaluation of staff is, of course, a major responsibility for any school administrator. Although we do not wish to suggest that educational supervision is virtually synonymous with teacher evaluation, it is hard to deny that evaluation of staff is a critical duty for anyone going into this field.

This chapter considers a very important issue, namely, how does an effective educational leader carry out evaluation responsibilities? Even more important, how does one evaluate within a framework defined in large measure by one's individual educational platform and a sincere desire and commitment to ensure that the needs of students remain firmly at the center of the circle? We will look at the types of evaluation that must be carried out regularly in schools, and also the possible objectives of each of these types of evaluation. We will also consider some traditional problems that exist in the field of educational evaluation. Most important, we will look at some of the ways that some of these problems may be addressed. As usual, we conclude with the expectation that you will be able to define a personal stance regarding evaluation as a plank in your educational platform, and we also look at how evaluation can be made consistent with the value of keeping students at the center.

Evaluation is simply the process of determining the worth—goodness or badness—of something. Blaine Worthen and James Sanders (1987) provided further explanations of the basic concepts of educational evaluation by noting,

> . . . in education, [evaluation] is the formal determination of the quality, effectiveness, or value of a program, product, process, objective, or curriculum. Evaluation uses inquiry and judgment issues, including: (1) determining standards for judging quality and deciding whether those standards should be relative or absolute; (2) collecting relevant information; and (3) applying the standards to determine quality. Evaluation can apply to either current or proposed enterprises. (p. 22)

Evaluation implies the existence and use of a criterion or standard to which "something" being evaluated can be compared to determine relative worth.

Evaluation differs from another term with which it is often confused, namely assessment, which describes a process of judging something with or without an external standard or guide. All evaluation is a form of assessment, but not all assessment is evaluation.

TYPES OF EVALUATION

There are three types of evaluation: diagnostic, formative, and summative.

Diagnostic Evaluation

Diagnostic evaluation is normally used to determine the beginning status or condition of something. It is carried out prior to the application or intervention or treatment to determine (1) what intervention or treatment may be necessary (as a physician diagnoses an illness to establish needed medical treatment), or (2) the nature of an object or person so that after the intervention is completed, its effectiveness can be assessed (as physical scientists note the nature of an environment before they conduct an experiment so they know what effect their experiment has had at its conclusion). Social scientists make use of this same research strategy that, in turn, increases the overall importance of precision in the conduct of diagnostic evaluation.

Provide some examples of how this type of evaluation is utilized on a regular basis in education.

_____

_____

_____

_____

_____

_____

Educational leaders frequently use diagnostic evaluation. They are called upon to suggest treatments, remedies, or approaches to "fixing" things that are going wrong in schools. In the same way that a physician uses diagnostic data to determine treatment, educational leaders are expected to prescribe solutions. Diagnostic evaluation also provides a picture of conditions before anything is done, so the effect of an intervention can be determined.

Formative Evaluation

Worthen and Sanders (1987) point out that "formative evaluation is conducted during the operation of a program to provide program directors evaluative information useful in improving the program (p. 34). Formative evaluation is used to gain intermittent feedback concerning the nature of some activity or practice while it is in progress. Activities can be evaluated many times. And feedback from this kind of evaluation is usually applied to whoever is in control of the activity being evaluated.

Can you think of examples of formative evaluation being used regularly in school settings?

Unfortunately, formative evaluation is the least frequently employed type of evaluation. When educational leaders do make use of it, they rarely follow through with sufficient feedback to teachers and others.

Formative evaluation implies that the project or activity being reviewed could be improved if properly analyzed and assessed. Educational leaders would do well to find more opportunities for formative evaluation procedures. Leaders need to become "sensors" or monitors of work in progress. They also need to develop the skills and strategies necessary to feed information gained in this way back to the teaching staff.

Summative Evaluation

"Summative evaluation is conducted at the end of a program to provide potential consumers with judgments about the program's worth or merit" (Worthen & Sanders, 1987, p. 34). Summative evaluation is the process of collecting data in order to make final decisions about the future status of whatever is being evaluated. It is the "last chance," the final point where an ultimate disposition regarding a person or thing is made. Data collected as part of summative evaluation is directed exclusively toward the goal of making final judgments.

Provide examples of where summative evaluation is frequently used in the field of education.

_____

_____

_____

_____

_____

_____

_____

Summative evaluation differs from diagnostic and formative evaluation precisely in its emphasis on finality. Because it represents an absolute endpoint or a final decision, summative evaluation typically carries with it a sense of anxiety and seriousness, whether or not these feelings are warranted.

OBJECTIVES OF EVALUATION

The four major educational areas most frequently evaluated are students, curricular programs, curricular materials (often evaluated as part of the curricular programs), and staff.

Student Evaluation

Students are evaluated almost continuously in most schools, and all three types of evaluation are employed. For example, special education teachers use multiple *diagnostic* techniques to determine the nature of individual learning needs so that future instruction can be directed more precisely. Standardized achievement tests are often used to determine baseline data needed to plan more effective future instruction.

Formative student evaluation is an ongoing practice in most schools. Teachers give "pop quizzes" precisely because they want to get some sense of how well students are learning during the course of instruction, and also to provide students hints concerning the teacher's expectations for student mastery of course content.

A typical example of *summative student evaluation* is the traditional final exam that concludes a marking period, the results of which are used to make a summary "pass/fail" decision for a student. Similar judgments are made at the end of instructional units in subject areas and at the end of the entire school year. More recently, accountability movements across the nation (and nationally through "No Child Left Behind" legislation) have made success on standardized achievement tests into prerequisites for movement up to higher grade levels, hence the term "high stakes testing."

In addition to the examples provided here, list some additional examples of the use of different types of evaluation to address student performance.

(Diagnostic evaluation)

_____

_____

_____

_____

_____

(Formative evaluation)

_____

_____

_____

_____

_____

(Summative evaluation)

_____

_____

_____

_____

_____

Curricular Programs and Materials Evaluation

Schools frequently assess the quality of their overall curriculum as well as the materials available to assist students in attaining the stated goals of the curriculum. Committees of teachers, administrators, and others may work together to review the adequacy of the curriculum and the books that fit it. These activities may best be classified as *diagnostic* in nature.

A school might also review a new textbook midway through a school year in which it is initially used. The results of that review would be used, not to decide whether to continue using the text, but rather to determine if it could be used more effectively. Do students need supplementary readings? A workbook? This "mid-course" evaluation is *formative.*

At the end of the school year, teachers and administrators who have suggested new curricular programs or products earlier in the year might reconvene to decide if their recommendations were effective. *Summative* evaluation would provide data to assist the committee in making its final decisions and recommendations.

What are some additional examples of curricular programs and materials evaluation?

(Diagnostic evaluation)

_____

_____

_____

_____

_____

(Formative evaluation)

_____

_____

_____

_____

_____

(Summative evaluation)

_____

_____

_____

_____

_____

Staff Evaluation

There is a false assumption that supervisory responsibilities in education begin and end with the evaluation of staff. This is clearly a major responsibility for educational leaders that causes a great deal of anxiety for both leaders and those being evaluated. However, it is far from the sole evaluative responsibility area for educational administrators and supervisors.

Traditional employment interviews carried out before individuals are hired by a school district are an example of *diagnostic* evaluation of staff. Other methods frequently used to determine if an individual is suited for a particular job include employment exams to determine basic competency, psychological profiles, or statewide teacher competency tests. Districts also review letters of recommendation, academic records, criminal background checks, and employment files from previous positions.

Formative evaluation of staff is one of he most poorly developed features of the entire range of supervisory responsibilities. Periodic evaluation designed to provide teachers and other school staff members with feedback to encourage better performance sounds like a reasonable and simple thing to do. In practice, however, constructive non-threatening feedback is not regularly provided. First, administrative and supervisory personnel are often not trained in this type of evaluation designed to provide "mid-course" correction and improvement. Second, when administrative personnel are expected to provide constructive feedback, it is generally intertwined with evaluation processes that have final judgment implications. For example, an inexperienced teacher may be told that he or she has problems with classroom management in a way that can be used to promote growth and personal learning. While that sounds like good practice, it is also impossible to divorce that type of feedback from the decision making process leading to termination or continuation of service. Ideally, formative feedback would be provided by individuals not directly involved with final "hire or fire" decisions. Unfortunately, most schools do not enjoy the resources that would enable this type of separation of duty to occur.

Finally, educational leaders are often perceived as engaging in summative evaluation of teachers and others. Principals, for example, are often required to make a specified number of formal in-class observations of teachers each year to ensure that competent instruction is taking place in their schools. If it is not, the consequence may be the non-renewal of a teacher. Current political mandates to "fix schools" make it increasingly clear that school leaders have a major ongoing responsibility to ensure somehow that only qualified teachers are actually employed to provide quality instruction. Increasingly gone are days when teachers who had achieved tenure or continuing contracts are virtually exempt from any for of true summative evaluation.

What additional examples can be provided of staff evaluation activity in the areas of diagnostic, formative, and summative evaluation?

(Diagnostic evaluation)

_____

_____

_____

_____

_____

(Formative evaluation)

_____

_____

_____

_____

_____

(Summative evaluation)

_____

_____

_____

_____

Problems and Issues in Educational Staff Evaluation

Staff evaluation presents some special concerns to every educational leader. On the one hand, it is accepted that, to improve practice, we need to determine the worth and effectiveness of that practice. On the other hand, most people are aware of the trauma that frequently surrounds discussions of evaluation. This paradox will never be resolved. But educational leaders may reduce tension by remaining aware of some common problems that cloud the practice of effective evaluation of personnel.

Mixing Purposes

Evaluation often suffers because the objectives of evaluation are mixed, particularly in terms of formative and summative evaluation. Formative evaluation demands a climate of openness and trust to exist between evaluator and those being evaluated so that deficiencies might be admitted and improvement can be focused. If school personnel suspect that information collected as part of formative evaluation will come back to haunt them during later summative evaluation, trust and openness are quickly destroyed. Consequently, leaders should strive to separate formative and summative evaluation as completely as possible, even to the extent of involving different people for different purposes. In recent years, peer coaching techniques have become increasingly popular in schools so that teachers, not administrators, are engaged in formative activity.

Have you seen examples of situations where the mixing of formative and summative staff evaluation has led to problems in any school on which you make have worked?

_____

_____

_____

_____

_____

_____

_____

Lack of Teacher Involvement

Teachers often report that they feel as if they have not had significant involvement in the development of district staff evaluation programs. While more school systems try to address this shortcoming by creating district evaluation committees to monitor and review practices and criteria used for evaluation, there are countervailing forces in effect. In Texas, for example, individual school districts theoretically may develop their own staff evaluation practices. But state laws and regulations are so restrictive that the vast majority (all but a handful of the state's more than 1,000 school districts) opt for the use of something called the Professional Development and Appraisal (PDAS) System promoted by the Texas Education Agency. Developing local versions of the same system is generally seen as a cost ineffective and time-wasting exercise. As more states believe that practices in this one large state are desirable, more places may move toward PDAS-like systems.

Another reality is seen in the opening scenario, where local boards of education begin to define their own needs for greater control and demand for accountability by requiring increasingly that staff evaluation be an administrative task focused almost exclusively on staff summative evaluation, carried out without "interference" from teachers and their associations.

How would you assess the involvement of teachers in the design and implementation of staff evaluation practices in your school or district?

_____

_____

_____

_____

_____

_____

_____

Lack of Self-Evaluation

Little consistent emphasis has been given to the concept of staff self-evaluation. The prevailing view suggests that evaluation is (or should be) "done to" staff by administrators and supervisors. However, the fact is that evaluation conducted by an individual reflecting on his or her performance is likely to be a much more powerful activity than any evaluation done by an external source.

To what extent is self-evaluation valued in staff evaluation practices that you have seen in your career?

_____

_____

_____

_____

_____

_____

Inadequate Evaluation Criteria

Criteria used for staff evaluation often come from the administrator's or supervisor's personal preferences. Some leadership personnel, for example, may tend to judge the effectiveness of teaching performance largely to the extent to which the teacher's activities may resemble how the leader would teach the same material. In fact, staff evaluation criteria and instruments should be based primarily (or exclusively) on the findings of teacher effectiveness research (Berliner & Tikunoff, 1976). It should also be noted that "effective teaching" is not limited to in-class instructional practice that appears correlated with higher student performance on standardized measures. There is also some evidence that supports the notion that the affect of a teacher may also impact significantly on student learning, although such effectiveness is much more difficult to "prove" with traditional research strategies. Reliance on such "feelings" that a teacher is carrying out effective instruction is often referred to as "artistic evaluation." Unfortunately, in today's climate of politically defined educational accountability, a perspective that includes feelings, perceptions, and artistic sensation is not always a popular stance.

How satisfied are you that the criteria used in the evaluation of teachers and teaching reflect what should be used in making summative judgment of effective performance? What might be some addition issues to be considered?

_____

_____

_____

_____

_____

_____

_____

Evaluation Procedures Not Communicated

Many school systems take great pains to improve the quality of their evaluation procedures. Often, such staff evaluation procedures are excellently "packaged." Yet attempts to make use of these programs fail because once new evaluation programs are designed, they are not sufficiently communicated to the entire staff of a school district. Districts frequently develop new evaluation procedures one year and then fail to "reeducate" staff about these procedures in following years, assuming that "we all know about those practices around here." Unfortunately, that assumption is often incorrect.

To what extent do you believe that the teachers and staff of your school are aware of the evaluation procedures that are being used?

_____

_____

_____

_____

_____

_____

_____

Insufficient Expertise

Effective staff evaluation often suffers because the administrative or supervisory staff called upon to implement these procedures may lack sufficient technical expertise in the area of evaluation. Those who have a background in this area tend to have had specific training primarily in summative evaluation procedures, often to assist administrators in avoiding legal problems that may arise on staff termination cases. Formative evaluation is rarely seen as an activity that calls for special attention.

To what extent are you satisfied that administrative and supervisory personnel are sufficiently well-versed in the effective use of formative and summative evaluation procedures in your school or district?

_____

_____

_____

_____

_____

_____

As you consider these various problems associated with the effective use of staff evaluation procedures in education, return to the scenario that opened this chapter. How many of the problems listed here do you anticipate becoming problems that might face the administrative and supervisory staff of Melisssa's school and school district?

_____

_____

_____

_____

_____

_____

Review the types of evaluation and the objectives for evaluation that are noted in this chapter. What would you advise Melissa as she prepares to become the evaluator of teachers this next school year?

_____

_____

_____

_____

_____

_____

BUILDING YOUR EDUCATIONAL PLATFORM

How you carry out your duties as an educational leader in the area of evaluation depends on many factors. One of these is your knowledge regarding effective (and legal) evaluation techniques. Another issue concerns your awareness of local policies, practices, and ultimately legal issues facing administrative and supervisory personnel. You also need to understand less formal sources of information, including local history, tradition, and political issues. But above all, effective evaluation will depend in large measure on your individual values and perspective related to this area. Your personal platform can be an important guide to help you.

In your point of view, what is the primary purpose of staff evaluation that is carried out in a school or district?

_____

_____

_____

_____

_____

_____

How consistent are local policies and expectations for evaluation with your personal understanding of evaluation of personnel?

_____

_____

_____

_____

_____

_____

_____

KEEPING STUDENTS AT THE CENTER

How the evaluation of programs, teachers, and students is carried out in a school can serve as a strong indicator of how committed a school is to the vision of ensuring that students are kept in the center of efforts made in a school.

Diagnostic evaluation of candidates for teaching positions may assist you in determining what the goals and objectives of a future may be. Asking applicants for information concerning their personal platform can go a long way to ensuring that your teachers will be focused on students' needs rather than simple satisfaction of personal wishes and goals. Simply hearing a job applicant espouse commitment to "standards" means little is you cannot determine for whom the standards are being developed.

Using formative evaluation can be helpful, too. As the school year progresses, it can be important to keep using commitment to student needs as a kind of litmus test throughout a school year. It is natural for teachers and staff to "take their eye off the ball from time to time" and ignore long-term dedication to serving students. Formative evaluation can be an important way to remind people on occasion the primary reason for schools to exist in the first place.

Finally, in the worst cases, summative evaluation can be used as the ultimate way to keep a staff committed to service to students. If that is a driving goal for a school, it can be reinforced by utilizing service to students as a characteristic to be sought when tough decisions about keeping or terminating teacher must occur.

IN REVIEW

There is more to supervision than evaluation. But evaluation is a major responsibility for anyone in a role as an educational leader. This chapter presented information about more than the use of summative staff evaluation—often the only aspect of evaluation considered. In addition, evaluation must be carried out concerning curriculum and students as well. And different types of evaluation are possible: diagnostic formative, and of course, summative evaluation.

Regardless of the type of evaluation or the objectives of the evaluative process, two additional important issues must be recalled with regard to discussions of educational evaluation. First, the individual educational platform of the educational leader will have a great deal to do with exactly how evaluation is carried out, and for what purposes. Second, there may be no more powerful issue to be considered than the evaluation of programs and people as a way to preserve the central focus of any good school, namely the ways in which focus and attention can be maintained on student needs.

REFERENCES

Berliner, D., Tikunoff, W. (1976). The California Beginning Teacher Evaluation Study: Overview of the ethnographic study. *Journal of Teacher Education, 27,* 145–159.

Scriven, M. (1967). The methodology of evaluation. In R. E. Stake (Ed.), *Curriculum evaluation.* American Educational Research Association Monograph Series on Evaluation. Chicago: Rand McNally.

Worthen, B. R., & Sanders, J. R. (1987). *Educational evaluation: Alternative approaches and practical guidelines.* White Plains, NY: Longman.

8 Defining "Effective" Leadership Practice

The new principal at Terwilliger Elementary School is Burt Aimsley. He has been a principal for ten years at two other schools in another state. He and his wife recently moved to the Dallas area to escape the winters of the northeast. It was also a chance for Betty to be closer to her father and two sisters, all of whom lived around Austin. Although the salary levels were considerably lower in Texas than they were in Massachusetts, the Aimsleys were happy with their choice. Besides, Burt was now able to tap into his Massachusetts retirement account, and so he was more than sufficiently compensated for the move.

Burt was particularly interested in taking on the challenges associated with leading a school in a state that had gained a great deal of national visibility because of its efforts to address accountability in schools. The system, as Burt understood it through his reading and correspondence with colleagues in his new state, was brilliant in its construction. Everything hinged upon the state's mandated "Texas Essential Knowledge and Skills" or TEKS. This is the state's curriculum for all subject areas in all grade levels. It was the strongest model seen across the country for an effort to ensure that there was some guaranteed substance in classrooms. Burt came from years of experience where he realized that, in many cases, students were likely to learn only if the individual teachers were willing to cover material of substance. He grew weary of finding unevenness in his teachers' commitment to covering material in their classes. To be sure, he had the pleasure over the years of working with many teachers who were absolutely great educators. They went well beyond the local district's curriculum guides to make certain that students acquired basic levels of information, and they went way beyond those minimal expectations. But he also had a great deal of experience with teachers who gave the district curriculum only a passing glance as they spent most of their class time teaching whatever they wanted to teach whenever they felt like teaching it. Things were getting better in New England, but no state in that region had yet achieved the level of high expectations that schools in Texas demonstrated.

Now that he was in Texas, he could truly understand the system even better than he could as an outsider. He saw the tight connection between the TEKS and student performance expectations on the annual statewide achievement tests (TAKS). Students had to pass these tests in Grades 3, 5, 7, 8, 10, and 11. Failure to demonstrate mastery in Grades 3 and 5 meant possible non-promotion to Grades 4 and 6, while failure in high school could deprive students of the opportunity to graduate. It was a tough set of standards, but again, Burt thought that the system was far ahead of some of what he had seen in other areas of the country.

At the first full faculty meeting in August at Terwilliger, Burt spent a bit of time telling the teachers about his past experiences. He said that he hoped that teachers had the patience to understand his accent, and he promised people that he would soon be saying "Y'all" and "Fixin' to" while he strutted the halls in his new cowboy boots. But he also warned that he would probably never give up his Red Sox cap and homesickness when he saw Fenway Park on television. He also explained how enthusiastic he was about the prospect of working in a state that was so serious about ensuring quality education for students. He had spent quite a bit of time looking at the scores at Terwilliger, and he knew that he had landed in one of the best elementary schools in that part of Texas. The school had received an "Exemplary" ranking for the past two years, meaning that an extremely high percentage of third and fifth graders had done very well on all sections of the TAKS tests each year. Also, attendance was very high, discipline referrals were low, and the school truly appeared to be a national and state model of effectiveness.

As he concluded his positive review of the programs at Terwilliger, he asked his new staff if they wanted to ask a question or comment. Many teachers were just waiting for the opening to do just that.

"Mr. Aimsley, we really look forward to working with you. It's clear that you have high expectations, you respect us and the kids, and you are enthusiastic," noted Tammy Finch, a well-respected third grade teacher who had been at the school for several years. "But I think you need to know that, although we think this place is a great school, it has little to do with the TAKS, the TEKS, or the state accountability system in general."

"Tammy's right, Mr. Aimsley," said Tom Ortega, another teacher who had worked at the school for several years. "We're glad that we get recognized as a good school every year, but I think you'll find out quickly that there are some good schools in this district that just don't get the awards that high test scores give you. In fact, you'll find that several teachers send their kids to other elementary schools in the district rather than here, to some extent because the other schools are not 'exemplary.'"

"That's very surprising, Mr. Ortega," responded Burt. "I thought that, above all, teachers would want their own children to go to a school that was really effective."

Ortega replied, "We do. But you'll learn soon enough that there are other definitions of 'effectiveness' beyond getting high scores and a prize from Austin."

The discussion continued along the same vein for quite a while. The general reaction that Burt heard from all but the newest teachers in the school was pride that Terwilliger had received recognition as a good school, but also a lot of people who seemed as if they were warning their new principal that he needed to do a little more observation and reflection about what was really happening in his new home.

✦ ✦ ✦

In the past few years, American public schools have become increasingly used as a kind of benchmark to determine how well society is progressing. Both professional educators and the lay community alike have become sensitive to the fact that the topic of quality education has become one of the central issues to be reviewed with vigor in the press and in school board meetings around the country. Politicians have made great strides toward ensuring their futures by hammering away at the problem in schools today, and then they have earned even more visibility by suggesting that they had "the answer" to making certain that schools were going to be fixed. Perhaps the ultimate example of this was the passage of the "No Child Left Behind" legislation at the national level in 2002. At the heart of this is the requirement that schools make certain to hire only highly qualified teachers and also the need for schools to document the fact that there has been demonstrable "Average Yearly Progress" made by all students in a school. If these and other conditions are not met, schools can be classified as performing at such low levels of acceptability that parents may withdraw their children and move them to more acceptable schools. Essentially, this would result in the closure of certain schools across the country that did not "measure up" to minimally acceptable performance standards.

The critical thing to note in these efforts to legislate more acceptable practices in public schools is the fact that, in all cases, "performance standards" are virtually the sole measure of school effectiveness. The message is basically, regardless of what goes on in any school, the "bottom line" will always be determined by whether or not students demonstrate that they have learned. And that demonstration will be through passing scores on standardized achievement tests. In other words, a school can do many interesting things throughout a school year, but acceptability and effectiveness are understood by the percentage of students who pass a test each year.

If someone were to ask you for your personal broad definition of what constitutes a "good school," what would you say?

_____

_____

_____

_____

_____

_____

There are many different ways to answer the question that was asked above. Some might say that the "good school" would do well on the state achievement test each year. Another person might say that good schools are those where all students graduate and graduates all go to college. Others might say good schools are ones where there is no violence, no truancy, and no other serious discipline problems.

The fact is, there are probably as many different answers to the question "What is a good school?" as there are people who read that question. There is yet another way to answer it, perhaps in a more personal way. If you have children of your own, what kinds of things would you like to see in a school where you might send your own kids? If you don't have your own children, can you imagine a school where you might send children if you did have any? How would that good school look?

_____

_____

_____

_____

_____

_____

_____

If someone were to visit your good school, what are some of the things they would likely see? For example, what would the students be doing as a person walked around the school? Not only in classrooms, but during class changes, in the playground, or cafeteria, or other places where kids might gather during the school day?

_____

_____

_____

_____

_____

_____

What about the teachers? What might they be doing in the good school? What would they not be doing?

_____

_____

_____

_____

_____

_____

What about the other adults (clerks, secretaries, cafeteria workers, custodians) in your good school? What would they be doing as you walked around?

_____

_____

_____

_____

_____

_____

Read over your descriptions of the things that you would expect to see people doing in your school. Are there any common themes that you would expect to see demonstrated by the students, teachers, and other workers?

_____

_____

_____

_____

_____

_____

What about the school itself? How would it look?

_____

_____

_____

_____

_____

_____

_____

This exercise might be a good thing for the principal in our opening scenario to use with his staff. While Burt may be excited about the prospect of working in a state with what he believes is a good way of determining school effectiveness, it is clear that his teachers do not have a similar belief. It would be an important thing to do something to open the conversation between the principal and teachers as soon as possible so that the school could develop its own vision of what a good school should be.

IS "GOOD" THE SAME THING AS "EFFECTIVE"?

Now that you have had a chance to reflect on the things that you would see as you walk around a school that is so good that your own children (or other children that you want to see succeed) would go there, there is an issue that you need to add to this discussion. Simply being viewed as a "good school" today is really not enough. Increasingly, society wants to see more tangible evidence that a school is actually productive and demonstrating that it is getting things done. In other words, it is not enough for most people to hear about subjective, personal "feelings" about whether a school is good or not. In the current results-oriented organizational climate ("Don't tell me what you like, show me results!"), saying that a school is good enough for your child is likely to be viewed by many as a "nice" thing to say, but it is not enough to prove effectiveness.

What are some of the quantitative measures that can be used to determine if your "good school" is really effective?

_____

_____

_____

_____

_____

_____

If you have listed such things as passing rates, achievement test scores, discipline referrals, graduation rates, and other similar issues, you have provided data that most state education agencies record each year. Go beyond those kinds of indicators and identify any other concrete indicators of whether a school is effective or not.

_____

_____

_____

_____

_____

_____

LIMITATIONS

While discussions of alternative ways of defining school effectiveness may be interesting, there is a problem with much of what may be suggested here. In reality, the stakeholders who have the strongest voice in defining school effectiveness are typically not professional educators. They are, in fact, laypersons who serve political roles. These may include local school board members, state legislators, United States senators, state governors, or as we have seen recently, even the President of the United States. None of these political bodies can afford to accept less than convincing evidence that schools are achieving the results that are desired by the public, or that warrant the public's financial support of the public schools. As a result, we need to be aware that many conversations by educators regarding the shortcomings of such measures as statewide testing will do little to change the reality of the current climate that seeks greater certainty regarding "effectiveness in public education."

This does not mean that the views of professional educators need to be limited, or that warranted criticism would necessarily cease. Instead, it should serve the educational leader with a bit of a warning. The way in which schools will be judged for the foreseeable future will be through "objective" measures such as testing, passing rates, college placements, and so forth. The responsibility of the educational leader will be to explain what such concrete indicators really mean. Even more important, your duty will be to explain what you are going to do in response to negative indicators that may appear. People do not want to hear excuses; they want explanations and plans for improvement.

Look at your present school in terms of the performance indicators that are regularly shared with the public. Locate any items that seem to suggest weaknesses in your school's programs. In the space below, do not provide explanations or excuses (e.g., "Our reading scores are low because we had a lot of students who do not speak English as their primary language taking the test this year.") Instead, provide statements that indicate what you plan to do to deal with the shortcomings that are shown by the data (e.g., "We will seek additional financial support for tutoring programs to assist our ESL students next year").

_____

_____

_____

_____

_____

_____

_____

BUILDING YOUR PERSONAL PLATFORM

There is little doubt that we are in an age of accountability for public schools. As a result, it is critical for anyone in an educational leadership role to give some serious thought to the issue of school effectiveness. In order to be an effective leader, you will need to be proactive in your work—anticipate demands and expectations before you are forced to respond completely to the will of others. It may be that your personal vision of effectiveness of schools may not match perfectly the definitions of success that are provided by others. But that does not mean that your only role is to accept all things as institutional givens. By having a clear idea of what constitutes effectiveness, you may not be able to change the inevitable demands from the outside world. However, your ability to create a vision may be an important way to provide an added value to the vision that can be attempted in your school. Remember that most accountability efforts are directed toward ensuring that minimal standards are met. Your job as a leader is to search for ways that go beyond the minimum.

As part of your educational platform, what statement would best described your personal vision of what constitutes effectiveness in a school?

_____

_____

_____

_____

_____

_____

_____

KEEPING STUDENTS AT THE CENTER

In a sense, the process of retaining a commitment to serving the needs of students can be viewed as an extremely strong statement of the effectiveness of any school. In other words, if you take care of the students, your school is effective. Unfortunately, popular discussions concerning the success of schools will not likely accept such a statement as proof of educational success.

But keeping your eye on the importance of student needs can serve as the ultimate benchmark of an effective schools if you also make certain to address the greater needs of students than those that are measured solely by the most politically popular methods now being used across the nation. If you want to serve students, do not remain limited to the attainment of minimums.

IN REVIEW

This chapter was meant to serve as a place where you could reflect on your own notions of what "effectiveness" in a school might be. There are, of course, no limitations on others who wish to suggest "what's wrong with schools." As a leader, you cannot be limited by such quick fixes and recipes. This chapter suggested quite strongly that effectiveness is always going to be an issue that educators must consider. It is impossible to remain fixed with attaining certain test scores or other indicators. Effective leadership keeps schools moving toward more and more important goals.

9 The Purpose of Schooling

Manny Hernandez and Mitzi Franklin were both starting their first year as principals in the Spudnut Valley local schools. They had come from other nearby districts, and both had extremely positive reputations as teachers, but relatively little experience as school administrators. Manny had been the director of a magnet program for high school students who were interested in careers in commercial aviation. His school was actually a former hangar at the community airport. As a result of his work, he had gained a great reputation in the business community, and also the respect of colleague educators who saw how he had the ability to work effectively with students who had little prior positive experience in schools.

Mitzi had a somewhat more conventional background on the way to the principalship. She had seven years of experience as a middle school teacher, then two and a half years as an assistant principal in that same school. Now, she and Manny were to become beginning principals in two middle schools that were part of the same high school feeder pattern. Manny went to East Clover Middle School while Mitzi took over at Upward Down. It was reassuring to both "rookies" that they would have an equally new colleague very close.

The proximity of the two schools and two new administrators was a coincidence that was quite fortunate in late October when both schools were to undergo reviews by teams of educators who came from the local university and other school districts to participate in what were called "School Improvement Reviews." Spudnut Valley had sponsored these visits every three years in each school in the district. All of the schools in the feeder zone with Upward Down and East Clover were due for the experience this year. About six weeks before the visit of the "School Improvement Review Committee," both Manny and Mitzi received calls from Dr. Woodford Firewalker, the associate dean of the education school at nearby Stateville College University who was designated as the chair of the site visit teams.

"The first thing I want to get out to all the reviewers is a brief statement of the history and general background of each of your schools," said Dr. Firewalker. "I want folks to get some sense of your communities, and also the general demographic characteristics of the schools. Many people have probably already been here over the years, but for the sake of everyone, I'd like a 'snapshot' to study in advance."

Both Mitzi and Manny knew that the chair would want something like that, so they had already put together some material.

"I'd also like you to send me a copy of your personal vision for your school," the professor continued. "Our visit will not have a lot to build on if we do not know what the leader expects."

Mitzi immediately started to think about what she expected at Upward Down over the next several months. Since the school was a Title 1 facility, and the majority of her students were minority students, her immediate thought was that it was critical to work toward the development of students' positive self-images, self-esteem, and general interest in education as a way to escape poverty. By contrast, Manny, as the principal of a school with a similar set of characteristics as Mitzi's saw things quite differently. "My kids need to learn how to read and write and how to demonstrate basic competence in math. Those will be the first steps toward a more successful life."

The two principals remarked at the fact that, although their schools were only a few blocks apart and served the same community in many ways, kids were likely to get a much different educational experience in the two schools. There was no arguing between the two novice administrators. Instead, there was a recognition that differences frequently produce greater outcomes, and so they agreed to disagree whenever there was a need to get more points of view out "on the table."

◆ ◆ ◆

There are many possible planks that can be a part of an educator's personal platform. There is no "perfect" format that contains all the possible values that are likely to impact on a leader's behaviors and what takes place in a school. Having said that, however, this is a strong suggestion to include a strong statement regarding what you personally believe are some of the major reasons for schooling in the first place. In fact, this issue is so critical that it might be the first plank in your platform or, as it is here, the last statement. After all, "why" you have schools in the first place is likely to have a major impact on virtually every other aspect of your professional belief system.

This chapter will lead you through a reflection related to what you view is the most critical purpose is for a school. Actually, while some alternative perspectives are described here, your own view may be a combination of two, three, or more of what is noted here, or your view may be completely apart from anything described here. Remember, however, that answering "why" questions frequently give meaning to all other answers.

As it has been the case in all previous chapters, this chapter will ask you to articulate your understanding of this topic as part of your platform. And you will also be asked to specify how an individualized perception of the purpose of schooling can be made consistent with the primary goal espoused throughout this book, namely putting students at the center of our work as educators.

ALTERNATIVE PURPOSES

There are probably as many specific answers to the question, "What is the purpose of schooling?" as there are people in the world. However, there have been some broad categories of responses that have served as the frameworks to respond to what may easily be the single most important question to guide a leader's actions and behaviors in schools. Here, five different frameworks are listed not to delimit you, but rather to provide a possible starting point for your individual statement of purpose.

Acquiring Basic Skills

For many, the ultimate purpose of formal education is best defined in terms of the acquisition of fundamental knowledge and skills. Normally, these "Basic Skills" have been defined as "Reading, Writing, and Mathematics." Another term frequently used to describe this purpose is "The Three R's"—readin,' 'ritin,' and 'rithmetic.' The underlying assumption seems to be that, if people are able to master certain fundamental processes, all later learning throughout life could be accomplished. Reading skills are needed to learn through books, writing skills are the basis for needed communication, and mathematics are the beginning of many life skills, including the ability to be paid and pay bills, decide personal budgets, calculate and measure, and other activities in which understanding addition, subtraction, multiplication, and division are critical.

Clearly, the view that mastery of basic skills can be defined as a critical focus for formal education is an idea that has been embraced by many, and for many years. The core curriculum of many schools comprises such subjects as "reading," and "language arts," and "mathematics" that are appropriate for each grade level. As accountability practices continue to become the central educational concern of many states (and across the United States in response to "No Child Left Behind" legislation), the definition of effective student learning appears increasingly to be defined as "demonstration of acceptable levels of performance in the basic skills," normally, reading, writing, and mathematics.

More recently, lists of the traditional school subjects which constitute basic skills have been expanded. Now, "basic skills" include social studies and some forms of physical science. These listings of basic skills appear to be determinants of effective learning at all levels of schooling, from elementary schools, to middle schools, to senior high schools.

In your judgment, are there additional traditional subjects that should also be included in lists of basic skills for students?

_____

_____

_____

_____

_____

_____

While the acquisition of basic skills represents a tempting definition of a vision for schooling, those who resist this approach are often quick to note two limitations of this perspective. One is related to something that your response to the previous question may have already addressed. While the majority of people might define basic skills in quite traditional terms ("The Three R's"), others might quickly include such issues as "effective use of technology," or even "consumer economic awareness." The list of competencies for anyone who will achieve success in the modern world may become nearly endless.

The second potential limitation to thinking of basic skills as the purpose of schooling may be the fact that it is extremely difficult to even answer questions such as these: How much learning skill acquisition is sufficient to represent effective learning? Should reading be judged by the number of books that are read? If so, at what measured skill level? Or, is knowledge to be demonstrated exclusively through successful completion of standardized achievement tests?

How do you personally assess the value of thinking of basic skills acquisition as the most important purpose of schooling?

_____

_____

_____

_____

_____

_____

Developing a Commitment to Ongoing Learning

Some suggest that learning about something (i.e., the basic skills) has a definite value. However, an even greater value of effective schooling may be that schools lead people to develop greater commitment to the overall process of continuing to learn—well after formal schooling experiences may have been concluded. The argument is that the development of a positive attitude or disposition toward a worthwhile goal is far more important than simply acquiring facts.

If this purpose is adopted by a school, certain practices will likely be more evident. For example, if the school is truly dedicated to learning for the sake of learning, one might observe more examples of teachers working toward the development of positive attitudes that reflect a consistent desire to continue education well after formal schooling has concluded. The end of courses, school years, or even formal schooling (i.e., at the graduation ceremonies of a high school) are described consistently to students only as steps on the way toward a more important goal. Some might describe this as an educational activity, not simply training to demonstrate certain measurable skills. After all, how can we "count" a "love of learning"?

How much would you support this belief that schooling is mostly a way to increase students' desire to learn throughout their lives?

_____

_____

_____

_____

_____

_____

_____

Developing a Strong Economy Based on Schooling

Here, the view is that effective schooling is directed mostly at the effort to develop increased levels of knowledge among students as a way to ensure future economic growth and development. Schooling is a matter if ensuring financial viability in the future of this country.

This is not an unreasonable assumption. Nations with stronger schools and better educated citizens tend to have stronger economies. People who have strong backgrounds in such fields as engineering, science, and mathematics are often very inventive and committed to greater entrepreneurial behavior that is tied to the development of stronger economic profiles. Consider the differences that exist between the economic development of the United States and members of the European Economic Union and what is likely to occur in the foreseeable future in Third World nations of Africa and Central America.

The curriculum in schools where economic development is seen as a driving force for schooling would include courses in such areas as marketing, personal economics, and analyses of capitalism. Of course, the basic skills noted earlier and the desire to continue to learn would not be goals that were totally unrelated to education. But the focus would most directly involve making certain that young people were educated so that they might contribute to the development and maintenance of a robust and productive national economy.

What values would you see in efforts to define effective schooling as a path to economic growth and development across the nation?

_____

_____

_____

_____

_____

_____

_____

Increasing Vocational Skills

A fourth definition of purpose for schooling concerns the reliance on formal education as a way to increase the skills that students will need to acquiring jobs in the future. While this view would be compatible with the focus noted earlier related to learning basic skills, this view would no doubt have less use for such "nonvocationally related" instruction as performing arts, and even advanced placement courses in foreign language, English, or even social studies. The curriculum of a school dedicated to vocational training would include such experiences as mechanics, construction, computer programming, and other learning experiences that could lead to the ability of students to become gainfully employed as a result of learning practical skills while in school. The overall effectiveness of any school might be determined in large measure by the number of school graduates who land jobs, keep them, and retain their positions for extended periods of time. "Learning for the sake of learning" might well be seen as an activity that is somewhat frivolous.

What is your assessment of the acquisition of practical vocational skills as a primary purpose of education?

_____

_____

_____

_____

_____

_____

Improving Social Conditions Through Education

The last broad categorization of educational purpose might be based on the view that effective education will serve as the foundation of changing society for the better. Here, students would learn of the ways in which they may become conduits to greater equity and fairness in society, and defenders of social justice as the primary goal of an educational system. In this perspective, education has relatively little value if it is not directed toward the solution of social issues of injustice or inequity.

In practical terms, the curriculum of a school where this point of view was honored would no doubt include many opportunities for service learning activities, where students would be expected to engage in work in communities as a way to to promote greater community development through service to disenfranchised populations. Instruction would be guided in large measure through the use of problem-based activity. Learning specific information (i.e., basic skills acquisition) would be of little value if it were not directly tied to the need to go forth into the "real world" to work toward the resolution of critical problems and issues. Learning for the purpose of lifelong learning would be important if the lifelong learning were somehow tied to a focus on social problem solving. Economic development, per se, would be of little or no concern to those with a commitment to social justice. So might the acquisition of practical skills that could be used in the immediate application of work-related activity.

To what extent would the focus on education resolve issues related to equity, equality, and social justice be consistent with your own perceptions of the purposes of schooling?

_____

_____

_____

_____

_____

_____

_____

DEVELOPING YOUR EDUCATIONAL PLATFORM

After all alternative perspectives are reviewed and considered, what is your personal view of the primary purpose for schooling?

_____

_____

_____

_____

_____

_____

_____

KEEPING STUDENTS AT THE CENTER

Regardless of what purpose for schooling you identify as most critical in your platform, it remains your duty to not think of the external agendas of schooling (for example, economic development or social justice) as the real focus of your effort. Rather, effectiveness as a school leader must ultimately come from the enduring commitment of the leader and others to remain faithful not to personal agendas, but rather to the greater need to serve students. If you believe learning must be used as the basis for political reform or economic development, it is important to keep that in perspective. Political reform, social justice, increasing basic skills, or whatever is identified as the most important focus of the school, please recall that the most critical issue must always be defined as absolute commitment to serve the students in your school.

IN REVIEW

This chapter led you through a review of a critical plank in your personal educational platform, namely a determination of the reasons for schools to exist in the first place. Several alternative and popular perspectives were introduced, but in the final analysis, it must be your duty to keep the needs of serving students as the most important purpose that can ever be identified for operating schools or school districts.

Index